Crochet Patterns for Babies

2nd Edition

41 Adorable Patterns for Baby Hats, Blankets, & Clothes!

by Kitty Moore

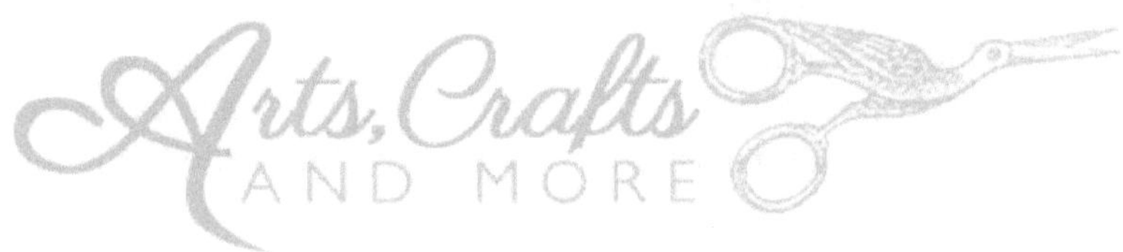

Table of Contents

Introduction ____ 5

1. Love Buttons Baby Blanket ___________________________ 6

2. Car Seat Blanket __________________________________ 8

3. Hooded Baby Blanket _______________________________ 10

4. Baby Sweater with Hood ____________________________ 14

5. Summer Dress _____________________________________ 20

6. Basic Baby Beanie _________________________________ 23

7. Hat Spikes ____ 26

8. Hat Flower ____ 29

9. Party Spirals for Hat ______________________________ 31

10. Bear Ears for Hat ________________________________ 33

11. Versatile Headband _______________________________ 35

12. Ring of Shells Headband ___________________________ 37

13. Nifty Newborn Leg Warmers ________________________ 39

14. Pacifier Clip _____________________________________ 41

15. Infant Mitts _____________________________________ 43

16. Tunisian Stitch Baby Bib __________________________ 45

17. Dress It Up Diaper Cover __________________________ 47

18. Baby Booties _____________________________________ 51

19. Happy Face Rattle ________________________________ 54

20. Diaper Wipes Wallet ______________________________ 59

21. Baby Wash Cloth _________________________________ 63

22. Baby Aviator Hat with Goggles _____________________ 65

23. Dragon Scale Baby Booties _________________________ 69

24. Textured Block Baby Blanket _________________________ 74

25. Swaddle Sack _________________________ 76

26. 2 Hour Baby Afghan _________________________ 78

27. Thick and Cozy Stroller Blanket _________________________ 80

28. Cozy Baby Sling _________________________ 82

29. Quick Baby Bib _________________________ 84

30. Cute Flower Pacifier Holders _________________________ 87

31. Easy Diaper Cover _________________________ 90

32. Primary Colors Block Blanket _________________________ 92

33. Baby Mittens with a Cord _________________________ 94

34. Owl Hat _________________________ 96

35. Bootie Knee Socks _________________________ 101

36. Soft Play and Nap Mat _________________________ 103

37. Thick and Quick Crib Blanket _________________________ 105

38. Baby Bottle Holder _________________________ 107

39. All-Natural Burp Cloth _________________________ 109

40. Crib Rail Guards _________________________ 111

41. Colorful Baby Blocks _________________________ 113

Final Words _________________________ 117

Disclaimer _________________________ 118

Introduction

The baby items you crochet are a legacy of love. They are keepsakes to be treasured because they are unique, heartfelt and handmade. The patterns in this book are the foundation that you individualize with your own color and style.

You may decide to crochet the basic beanie and add flowers or spikes or spirals. You may accept the challenge of the hooded sweater or simply enjoy the delicate beauty of the shell headband.

Whatever project you select, it will come alive in your hands as you make this very personal gift for a child.

1. Love Buttons Baby Blanket

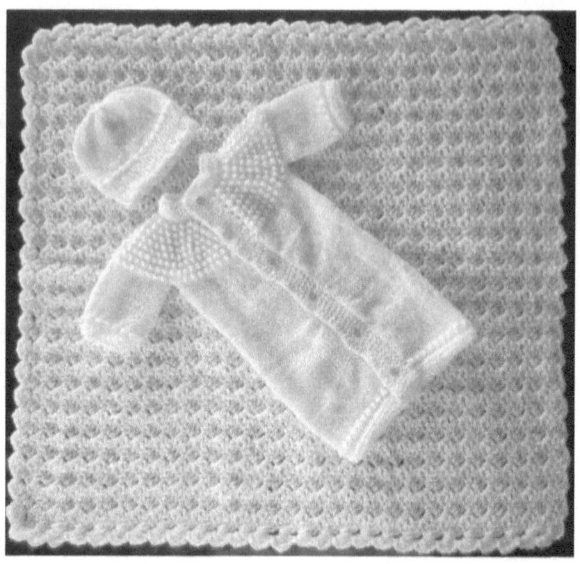

Materials

- 16 ounces - 4 ply soft yarn

- Crochet hook, size J/10; 6.0

Directions

1. Crochet chain of 99.

2. **Row 1**— In the 3rd chain, crochet 2 double crochets, skip 2 chains and start pattern: *slip stitch 1, chain 2, and double-crochet 2 stitches*. Repeat this pattern until the last three chains of the row. Then skip 2 chains, in last chain, slip stitch one, chain three. Turn.

3. **Row 2**— Double chain between chain 2 and 1st double chain. Continue pattern: *slip stitch 1, chain 2, and double-crochet 2 stitches.* Repeat to the end of the row. Crochet two chains and turn. Repeat Row 2 until your blanket is a square 32" x 32".

Blanket Edge

1. On all edges of the blanket, repeat pattern: *slip stitch 1, chain 2, double crochet 2 stitches.* Stitch 2 double crochets in each corner. Finish, weave in ends.

2. Car Seat Blanket

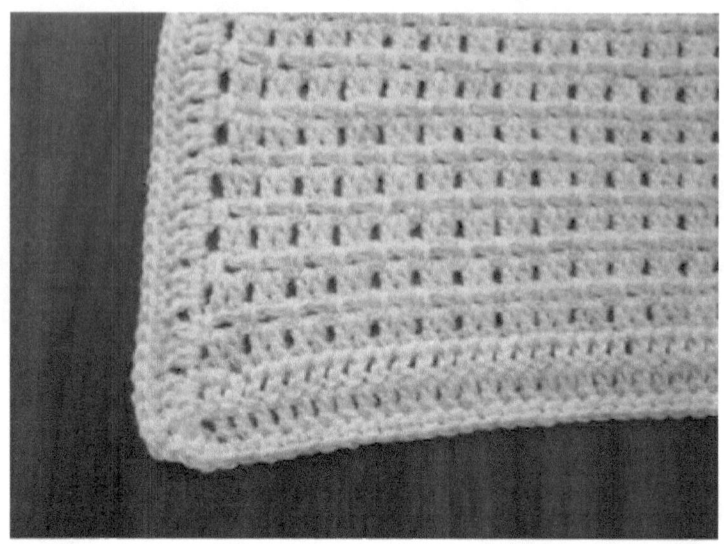

Materials

This small blanket is 19 inches x 23 inches

- One skein of sport-weight soft yarn

- Crochet hook G/6; 4.0

Directions

2. Chain 60.

3. **Row 1**— Double crochet in each stitch. Chain 1. Turn.

4. **Row 2**— Single crochet in 1st double crochet stitch. Chain 2, skip 2, double crochet, single chain in

space between next double crochet. Repeat this pattern for the rest of the row. Chain 1 and turn.

5. **Row 3**— Crochet 2 double crochet stitches in each double crochet. Double crochet in last single crochet. Chain 1 and turn.

6. Repeat Rows 2 and 3 until crocheted fabric is the length you want. End with Row 3 pattern. Chain 2 and turn.

7. **Last row**- Double crochet in each stitch and double crochet in turning chain. Chain 2 and turn.

Border

1. **Round 1**- Double crochet in each stitch around the sides of the blanket, with 3 double crochets in each corner. Join with a slip stitch.

2. **Round 2**- Single crochet in each stitch around the blanket with 3 single crochets in each corner. Finish off. Weave in ends.

3. Hooded Baby Blanket

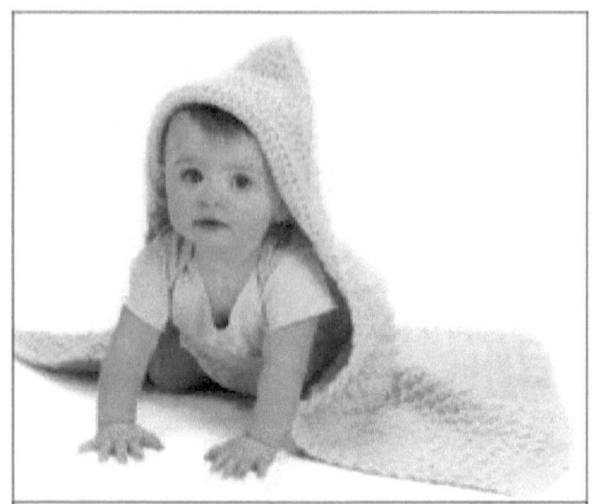

Materials

This blanket is 28 inches square

- 16 ounces 4-ply soft yarn

- Crochet hook J-10; 6.0

- Tapestry needle

Directions

Blanket

1. Chain 108 stitches. You will work Row 1 and Row 2 in a textured pattern until crocheted fabric measures 28 inches in length. Finish off. Weave ends.

2. Row 1— Crochet 2 double crochets into 3rd chain, skip 2 chains, crochet 1 single crochet stitch and 2

double crochets in next chain, skip next two chains, and repeat across row. Single crochet in last chain. Chain 2 and turn.

3. Row 2— Double crochet in first stitch, skip next two stitches, crochet 1 single crochet and 2 double crochets in next stitch, skip next 2 stitches, repeat across row. Single crochet in top of turning stitch.

Hood

1. Chain 4. **Row 1-** Crochet 2 double crochet stitches into 4th chain. Chain 3 and turn. **Row 2-** Crochet 2 double crochets in first stitch, 1 double crochet in next stitch, and crochet 3 double crochets in top of turn chain. You should have 7 double crochet stitches. Chain 3 and turn.

2. **Row 3-** Crochet 1 double crochet in first stitch and 1 double crochet in each stitch of the row. Crochet 2 double crochets in top of turning chain. You should have 9 double crochets. Chain 3 and turn.

3. **Row 4-** Crochet 2 double crochets in first stitch. Crochet 1 double crochet in each stitch of the row. Crochet 3 double crochets in top of turning chain. You should have 13 double crochets.

4. Repeat Rows 3 and 4 six times. You will have 49 double crochets. Place hood over one corner of the blanket, right sides together. Sew together with yarn and tapestry needle.

Blanket Trim

1. In contrasting color, or same color, single crochet every stitch at the edge of the blanket and hood. Stitch two single crochets in each corner. Finish off. Slip stitch to join. Weave in end.

I have included a bonus just for you…

FOR A LIMITED TIME ONLY – Get my best-selling book "DIY Crafts: The 100 Most Popular Crafts & Projects That Make Your Life Easier" absolutely FREE!

Readers who have downloaded the bonus book as well have seen the greatest changes in their crafting abilities and have expanded their repertoire of crafts – so it is *highly recommended* to get this bonus book today!

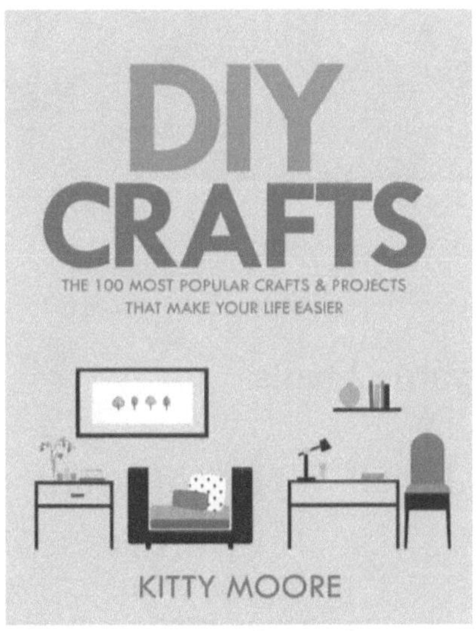

Get your free copy at:

ArtsCraftsAndMore.com/Bonus

4. Baby Sweater with Hood

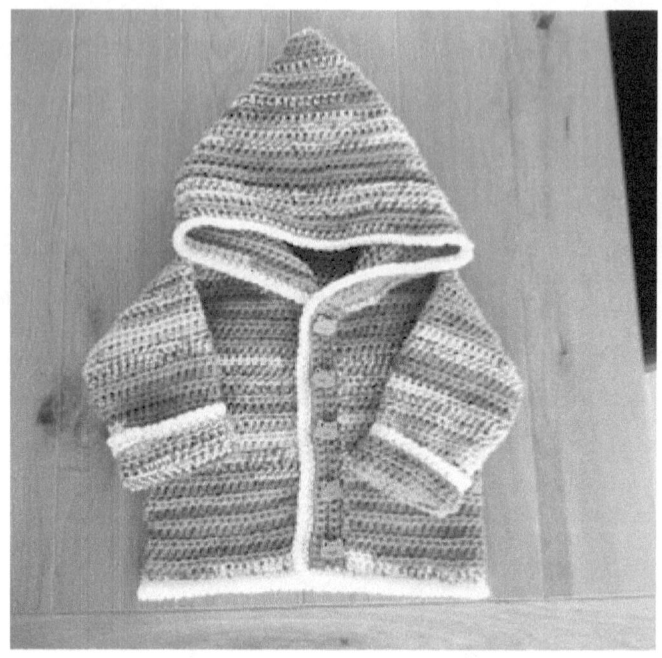

Materials

- 8-ply soft yarn, 2 balls

- Optional- 1 ball 8-ply soft yarn of a contrasting color

- Crochet hook, size H/8; 5.0

Directions

Note - Directions are for 6-month size, chest measurement 21 inches.

Back

1. Chain 41.

2. **Row 1**- Crochet 1 half-double crochet stitch in the third chain, and then crochet 1 half-double crochet stitch in remaining chains to the end of the row. Chain 2 and turn.

3. Repeat row 1, until material is 6 ½ inches long. Stop on right side, do not chain.

Shape Arm Holes

1. In the next row, slip stitch in the first four stitches. Chain 2. Crochet 1 half-double crochet in each stitch until last 4 stitches. Chain 2. Leave remaining stitches. You will have 31 stitches.

2. Continue until armhole measures 4½ inches. End with right side facing you. Do not chain. Fasten off.

Left Front

1. Chain 21.

2. Crochet 1 half-double crochet stitch in 3rd chain from the hook. Continue the row with 1 half-double crochet in each chain to the end. You will have 19 half- double crochets. Chain 2. Turn.

3. Repeat row 7 until material measures 6½ inches. End with right side facing you. Do not chain. Fasten off.

Shape Armhole

1. Slip stitch in each of first four stitches. Chain 2. Crochet 1 half-double crochet in each stitch of the row. Turn. Leave remaining stitches. You will have 15 stitches.

2. Continue until armhole measures 2½ inches ending with right side facing you.

Shape Neck

1. **Row 1**— Crochet 1 half-double crochet stitch in each stitch until the last 3 stitches. Chain 2. Turn. Leave remaining stitches. You have 12 half-double crochet stitches.

2. **Row 2**— Yarn over and draw up a loop in each of the first 2 stitches. Yarn over and draw through all the loops on the hook. Crochet 1 half double crochet in each stitch to the end of the row. Chain 2. Turn.

3. **Row 3**- Crochet one half double crochet in each stitch until the last 2 stitches. Half double crochet together over last 2 stitches. Chain 2 and turn. You will have 9 stitches.

4. **Row 4 and on**- Repeat row 2 until the length measures the same as back to shoulders. End with

right side facing. Omit chain at the end of the row. Fasten off.

Right Front

1. Crochet following Left Front directions. Reverse armhole shaping instructions.

Sleeves

1. Chain 29.

2. **Row 1**- Crochet 1, half-double crochet in 3rd chain from hook. Crochet 1 half-double crochet in each chain. Chain 2. Turn. You will have 27 half-double crochets.

3. **Row 2-3**- Crochet 1 half-double crochet in each stitch to the end or the row. Chain 2 and turn.

4. **Row 4**- Crochet 2 half-double crochets in 1st stitch and 1 half-double crochets until last stitch. Crochet 2 half-double crochets in last stitch. Chain 2 and turn. You should have 33 stitches.

5. **Row 5, 6, 7**- Repeat row 4.

6. Repeat rows 1-4, two times. Continue until work measures 7 ½ inches. Mark the end of the last row. Fasten off.

Hood

1. Chain 77.

2. **Row 1**- Crochet 1 half-double crochet in 3rd chain from hook. Crochet 1 half-double crochet in each chain. Chain 2. Turn. You will have 75 half-double crochets.

3. **Next 3 rows**- Crochet 1 half-double chain in each stitch to the end or the row. Chain 2 and turn.

4. **Row 4**- Half-double crochet over first two stitches. 1 half-double crochet in each stitch until last 2 stitches. Chain 2 and turn.

5. Repeat Row 4 until you have 59 stitches and material measures 6 ¼ inches. End with right side facing and no ending chain.

6. **Next 6 rows**- You will shape the back of the hood by slip stitching in the first three stitches of the next six rows. Crochet 1 half double crochet in each stitch to last 3 stitches. Turn leave remaining stitches. You will have 23 stitches. Fasten off.

Edging

1. With the same color or a contrasting color, slip stitch around the outer edge of the jacket, working 3 stitches into each corner. Then crochet one single crochet stitch into each chain, with three single crochet stitches in each corner.

Sewing Sweater Together

1. Sew sleeves along armhole edges of front and back. Sew side and sleeve seams. At the base of each sleeve, reverse the sewing to allow a 2-inch turnback at the base of sleeve.

5. Summer Dress

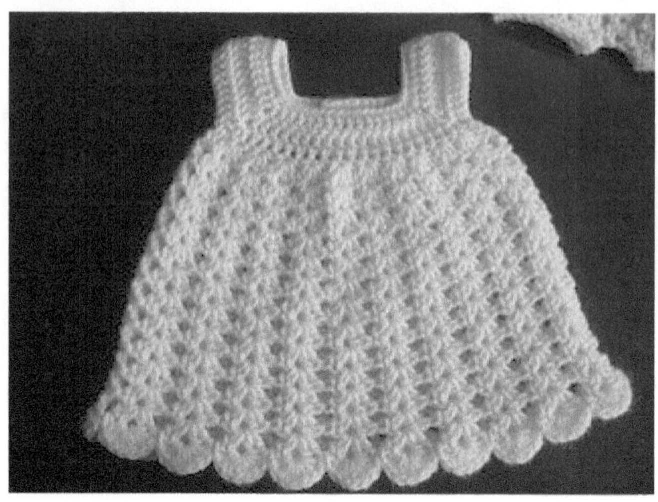

Materials

This dress is for babies 3-6 months

- Light weight 8/ply soft yarn

- Crochet hook H/8; 5.00

Directions

1. **Special Stitch used V Stitch**— double crochet, chain 1, double crochet all in the same spot. **Row 1–** Chain 68. This row will show you the shape of the dress. **Back-** Double crochet 1 in 3rd chain, crochet 1 double crochet stitch in the next 8 chains. V stitch in the next chain, double crochet in the next 15 chains. V stitch the next chain.

2. **Shoulder-** Double crochet in the next 15 chains. V stitch in the next chain. **Front-** Double chain in the next 15 chains, V stitch in the next chain. **Shoulder-** Double chain in the next 7 chains, chain 3 and turn. **Row 2—** Double crochet into 2nd double crochet from the end. Chain 3. Double crochet in the next 6 double crochets. V stitch in the chain 1 center of the V stitch. Double crochet in the next 17 double crochets.

3. V stitch into the chain 1 center of the V stitch. Double crochet into the next 17 double crochets. V stitch into the chain 1 center of the V stitch, double crochet into the next 11 double crochets, chain 3 and turn. **Row 3—** Double crochet into 2nd double crochet from the end. Double crochet in the next 12 double crochets. V stitch in the chain 1 center of the V stitch.

4. Double crochet in the next 19 double crochets. V stitch into the chain 1 center of the V stitch. Double crochet into the next 19 double crochets. V stitch into the chain 1 center of the V stitch, double crochet into the next 9 double crochets, chain 3 and turn. **Row 4—** Double crochet into 1st double crochet. *Skip 1, 2 double crochets, chain 1, 2 double crochets.* Follow this pattern 4 times.

5. Crochet 2 double crochets into chain one center of V stitch, chain 1, crochet 2 double crochets into next V stitch center, forming the arm hole as you skip 19 double crochets. *Skip 1, 2 double crochets, chain 1, 2 double crochets.* Follow this pattern 10 times.

Crochet 2 double crochets into the center of the V stitch, chain 1. Crochet 2 double crochets into next V center stitch. This forms the second arm hole.

6. *Skip 1, 2 double crochets, chain 1, 2 double crochets* 4 times. Skip 1, double crochet into the next stitch. There will be 3 stitches left. This is the button tab. Single crochet 1 and slip stitch join to the other 2 double crochets. Chain 3 **but do not turn.** The rest of the pattern will be crocheted in the round. Double crochet 1, chain 1, and 2 double crochets to join chain 1 of each set all the way around the dress. You should have 21 sets. Slip stitch to join last and first sets.

7. **Row 6-16**— Chain 3, double crochet 1, chain 1, 2 double crochets to join. *2 double crochets, chain 1, 2 double crochets* into the chain 1 of each set all the way around. Slip stitch to center of the set. Repeat 10 times. Slip stitch between set joins and make a shell of 7 double crochets in the center of the set. Slip stitch in between. You will have a total of 21 shells.

Finishing

1. Single crochet around the neck and armholes in the same or contrasting color.

2. Add buttons to the front or back of the dress.

6. Basic Baby Beanie

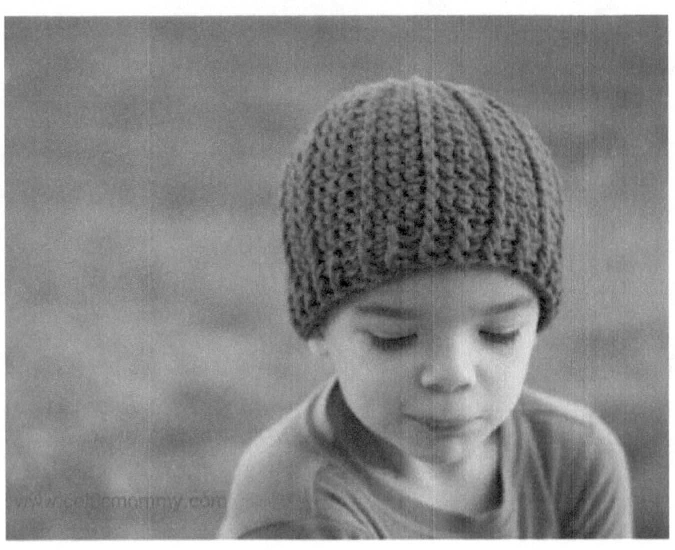

Materials

Directions are for two sizes of hat- a small hat for children 2-4 years old and a larger hat for children 4-12 years old

- Worsted weight yarn

- Crochet hook, size H/8; 6

- Tapestry Needle

Directions

1. **Round 1-** Chain 3. Crochet 13 double crochets in first chain. Join with a slip stitch to the top of the chain. You will have 14 stitches.

2. **Round 2-** Chain 2. Crochet 1 forward post double crochet. Crochet 1 double crochet stitch in each stitch in the round. Join with a slip stitch to the top of the chain. You will have 28 stitches.

3. **Round 3-** Chain 2. Crochet in each forward post double chain. Crochet 1 double crochet stitch in each stitch in the round. Join with a slip stitch to the top of the chain. You will have 28 stitches.

4. **Round 4-** Chain 2. Crochet in each forward post double chain. Crochet 2 double crochet stitches in each stitch in the round. Join with a slip stitch to the top of the chain. You will have 42 stitches.

5. **Round 5-** Chain 2. Crochet in each forward post double crochet. Crochet double crochet stitches on top of forward post double chain. Join with a slip stitch to the top of the chain. You will have 56 stitches.

6. **Round 6-** Chain 2. Crochet in each forward post double crochet. Crochet double crochet in each double crochet. Repeat the round. Join with a slip stitch to the top of the chain. You will have 56 stitches.

7. For small size hat, repeat Round 6 for Round 7-14. For larger hat, repeat Round 6 for Round 16-18,

Finish

1. Crochet one forward post double chain in the forward post double chain. Then *forward post in double chain, back post in double chain.* Repeat this pattern for the round. Join with a slip stitch at the end of the row. Finish off.

7. Hat Spikes

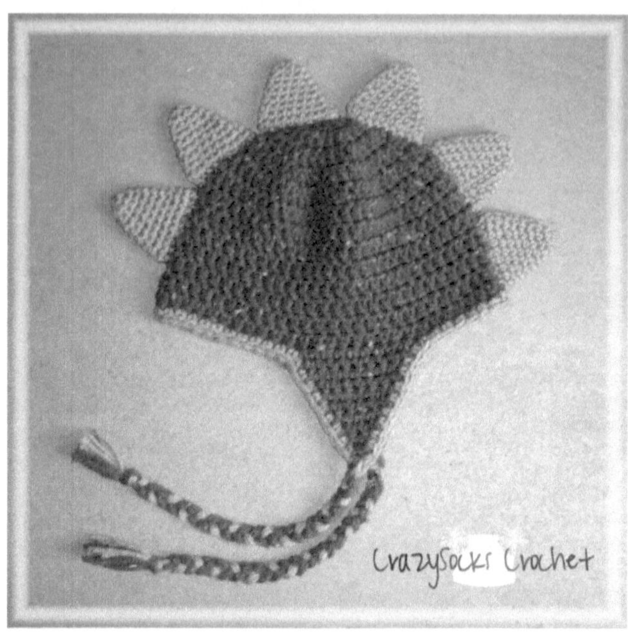

Materials

- Weighted Worsted Yarn

- Crochet hook, size G/6; 4.0

- Yarn needle

Directions

Note- This pattern is for one spike. Repeat to make the number of spikes that you want to add to your hat.

1. **Round 1**- Crochet 3. Slip stitch to join round. Chain 1. Single crochet 6 stitches into the round. You now have 6 stitches.

2. **Round 2**- *Crochet 1 single crochet in the first stitch, single crochet two into the next stitch.* Continue this pattern for the rest of the round. You will have 9 stitches.

3. **Round 3**- Crochet 1 single crochet into each stitch for the rest of the round. You will have 9 stitches.

4. **Round 4**- *Crochet 1 single crochet into next two stitches, single crochet two stitches into next stitch.* Continue this pattern for the rest of the round. You will have 12 stitches.

5. **Round 5**- Crochet 1 single crochet into each stitch for the rest of the round. You will have 12 stitches.

6. **Round 6**- *Crochet 1 single crochet into first three stitches, single crochet two stitches into next stitch.* Continue this pattern for the rest of the round. You will have 15 stitches.

7. **Round 7**- Crochet 1 single crochet into each stitch for the rest of the round. You will have 15 stitches.

8. **Round 8**- *Crochet 1 single crochet into first four stitches, single crochet two into next stitch,* and continue this pattern for the rest of the round. You will have 18 stitches.

9. **Round 9**- Crochet 1 single crochet into each stitch
   for the rest of the round. You will have 18 stitches.
   Slip stitch into next single crochet. Fasten off. Leave
   a 6-inch length of yarn to attach the spike to the hat.

Attaching Spikes

1. Arrange completed spikes down the outside center
   of the hat. Use the 6-inch length of yarn to securely
   attach each spike on the inside.

8. Hat Flower

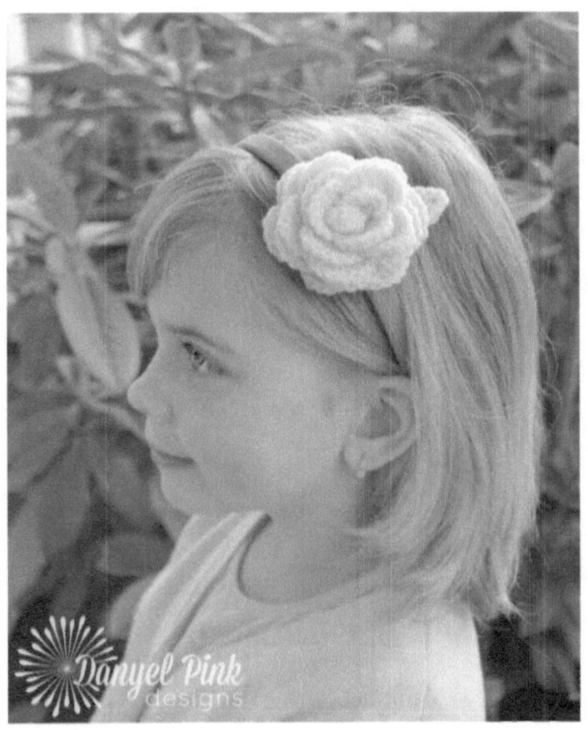

Materials

- Light weight yarn, any color

- Crochet hook, size G/6; 4.0

- Yarn needle

Directions

These directions will make one rose. Repeat to make the number of roses that you want for your hat.

Tip- This hat uses a **V** stitch. A **V** stitch is worked in one space. It consists of one double crochet stitch, 1 chain and 1 more double crochet.

1. **Row 1-** Crochet a chain of 45. In the third chain, complete a V stitch, and then *chain 1, skip 1, V stitch in next chain.* This pattern will be used for the rest of the row. Chain 1 and turn. You will have 21 V stitches.

2. Crochet 7 double crochets into V stitch. *Slip stitch into chain, skip one, chain one, 7 double chains into V stitch*, repeat until the last 2 V stitches. Slip stitch into chain 1 space, chain 1, 6 half-double crochet stitches into V space, slip stitch into chain 1 space, crochet 5 half double crochet stitches into last v space, slip stich to beginning chain.

Fasten off

1. Leave long length of yarn for sewing. You will have 21 petals.

2. Carefully roll the petals so that they radiate from the center out. Sew the bottom of the petals together to hold the shape.

9. Party Spirals for Hat

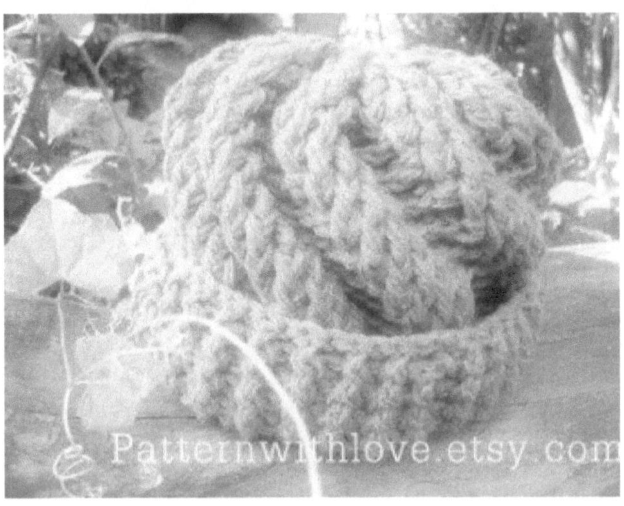

Materials

- Any yarn

- Any hook

- Crochet needle

Directions

This pattern will make one spiral. Change colors and make as many spirals as you want for your hat.

1. Crochet a chain of 25. In the third chain from the crochet hook, double crochet 7 stitches.

2. In the next chain, double crochet 8 stitches.

3. In the next chain, double crochet 8 stitches. Continue to the end of the chain.

Finish off

1. Leave a 6-inch tail to attach spiral to hat.

2. Position spirals to the very top of the hat. Sew 6-inch tail to the inside of the hat. Weave ends.

10. Bear Ears for Hat

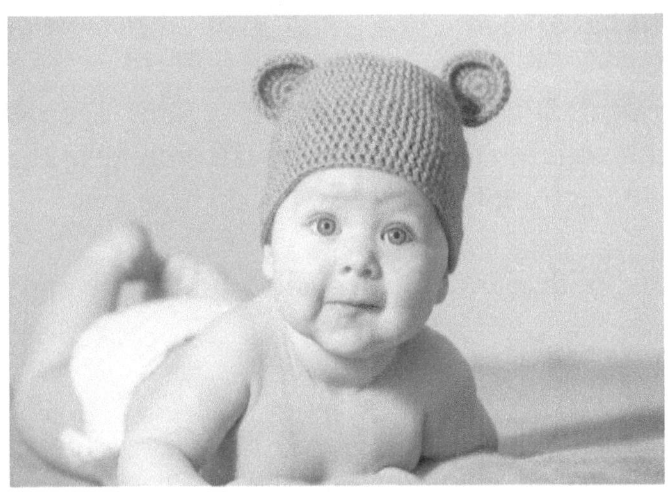

Materials

- Medium worsted weight yarn

- Crochet hook H/8; 5.0

- Crochet needle

Directions

Make two ears.

1. Chain 4. Slip stitch ends to form ring.

2. **Round 1-** Chain 1. Crochet 8 single crochet stitches into ring. Slip stitch to join. You will have 8 stitches.

3. **Round 2-** Chain 1. Crochet 2 single crochets into each single crochet stitch. Slip stitch to join. You will have 16 stitches.

4. **Round 3-** Chain 1. Crochet 1 single crochet into each stitch. You will have 16 stitches. Finish off. Leave a long tail of yarn.

5. Sew both ears to each side of the beanie. Weave ends.

11. Versatile Headband

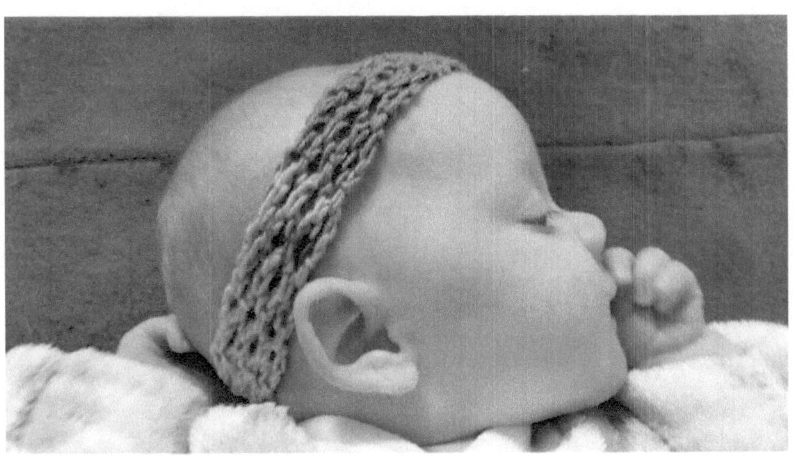

Materials

- Any yarn

- Any hook

Directions

Measure the size of the head that you are making the head band for baby to adult. Follow this pattern until you reach the desired length.

1. Chain 11.

2. **Row 1-** Slip stitch into the 5th chain. Chain 2. Skip 2. Slip stitch into the next chain. Chain 3. Skip 2. Slip stitch into the next chain. Chain 4. Turn. You will have 4 ovals in this row.

3. **Row 2**- Slip stitch into 3rd chain. Chain 3. Slip stitch into chain 2nd space. Chain 3. Slip stitch into last chain space. Chain 4. Turn. You will have 3 ovals in this row.

4. **Row 3**- Slip stitch into 4th chain stitch. Chain 3. Slip stitch into 3rd chain space. Chain 4. Slip stitch into 4th chain space. Chain 4. Turn. You will have 3 ovals in this row.

5. Repeat Row 3 until you crocheted your headband to the desired length.

6. Place right sides together. Join with a slip stitch.

7. Turn right side our and your headband is ready!

12. Ring of Shells Headband

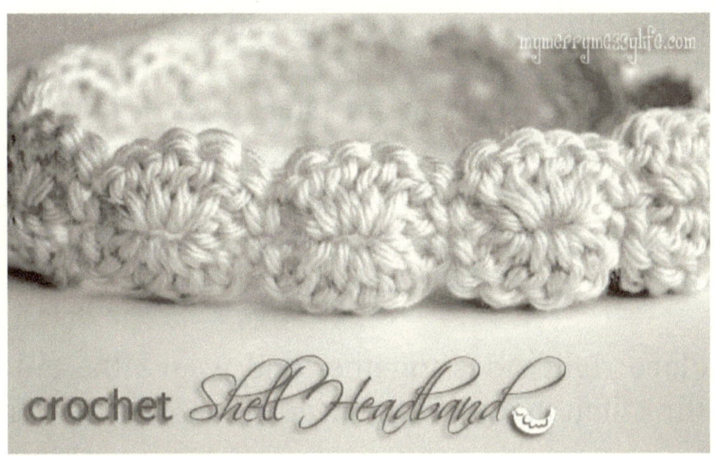

Materials

- 4-ply worsted weight soft yarn

- Crochet hook, size H/8; 6

Directions

These directions are for a six-month-old child. To make a larger or smaller headband, measure the head that you are making the headband for and crochet chains in step 1 to the desired length. The number of chains must be divisible by 4.

1. Crochet 44 loose chains.

2. **Pattern-** In the third chain, crochet 3 double crochet stitches in the same chain. Skip a chain, slip stitch in the next chain, skip a chain, crochet 4 double

crochet stitches in the next chain, skip a chain, and crochet 4 double-crochets stitches in the next chain. Repeat this pattern until the end of the chain. Turn.

3. Repeat the pattern in step two, but this time, crocheting into the lower loop of the original chain. The emerging pattern should be a symmetrical ring of shells on the top and bottom or the chains. Fasten off leaving a 6-inch tail.

4. Place right sides together and weave the tail into a slip stitch that joins the headband. Weave in end.

5. Turn right side out.

13. Nifty Newborn Leg Warmers

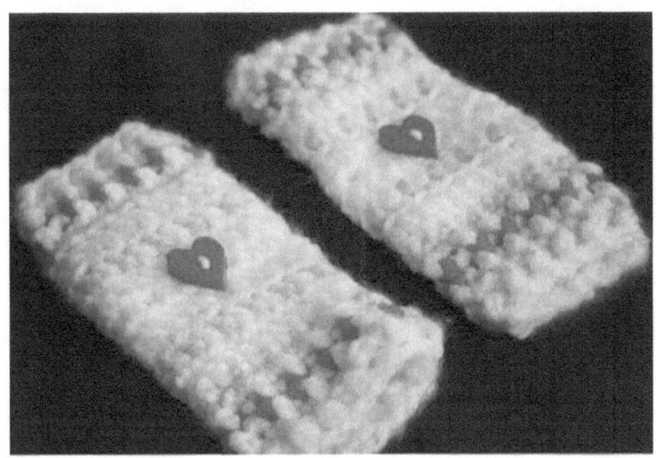

Materials

Size- Newborn

- 8-ply soft yarn, 2 balls

- Crochet hook, size J/ 10; 4

Directions

Tip - Special stitch for this pattern, cluster stitch. Yarn over, insert hook in next stitch, yarn over, and pull yarn through the stitch, yarn over again and pull yarn through two loops on the hook, repeat these steps three times. Yarn over draw yarn through 5 loops. This is a completed cluster stitch.

You will need to make two leg warmers.

1. Chain 20. Join with slip stitch to first chain to make a round. **Round 1**- Chain 3, double crochet the round. Join to the top of chain 3 with a slip stitch. You will have 20 double crochet stitches.

2. **Round 2**- Chain 2. Forward post around the first double crochet, back post around the 2nd double crochet. Continue this pattern for the rest of the round. Slip stitch to the fist forward post double chain. You will have 20 double crochet stitches.

3. **Round 3, 4**- Repeat round 2. You will have 20 double crochet stitches. **Round 5**- Chain 3, double crochet in each stich in the round. Join with a slip stich to top of chain 3. You will have 20 double crochets.

4. **Round 6**- Chain 3, cluster stitch in next double crochet, double crochet in next 3 double crochets, cluster in next double crochet. Complete this pattern for the round. Join with a slip stitch in the top of chain 3. You will have 5 clusters and 15 double crochets.

5. **Round 7 and 8**- Repeat round 5. **Round 9 and 10**- Repeat round 3. **Round 11**- Repeat the pattern of round 5.

6. **Round 12**- Repeat the pattern of round 6. **Round 13 and 14**- Repeat round 5. **Round 15-17**- Repeat round 3. Tie off.

14. Pacifier Clip

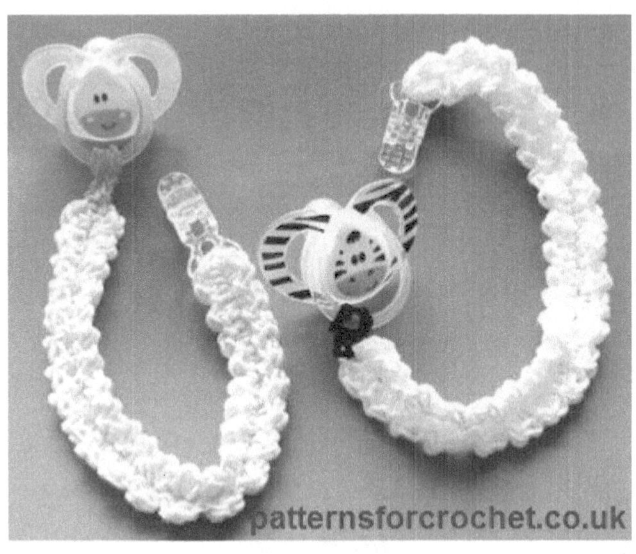

Materials

- Worsted weight cotton

- Optional - 1 ball 8-ply soft yarn of a contrasting color

- Crochet hook G/6; 4.00

- 4.00 Pacifier Clip

- Pacifier

Directions

1. Chain 46.

Side 1

1. Slip stitch in 2nd chain from hook. *Crochet 2 double crochet stitches in next chain, slip stitch in next chain.* Continue this pattern until last 2 chains. Crochet two double crochet stitches in next to last chain. In last chain, crochet one single crochet stitch, chain 6, crochet 1 single crochet stitch in 2nd chain from hook, and crochet 1 single crochet in the next 4 chains.

Side 2

1. Now you will work on the opposite side of chain. *Slip stitch in 2nd chain from hook, crochet 2 double crochet stitches in next chain, slip stitch in next chain.* Continue this pattern to last two chains. Crochet 2 double crochets stitches in the next to last chain. In the last chain, crochet one single crochet stitch, and then chain 6. Crochet 1 single crochet in 2nd chain from hook, 1 single crochet in next 4 chains, and then one single crochet.

2. Chain 14. Slip stitch to base of chain 14. This makes a loop.

3. Loop the pacifier through the loop end of Side 2. Attach the pacifier clip to the single crochet end of Side 1. Thread clip through single crocheted piece and secure with spare yarn.

15. Infant Mitts

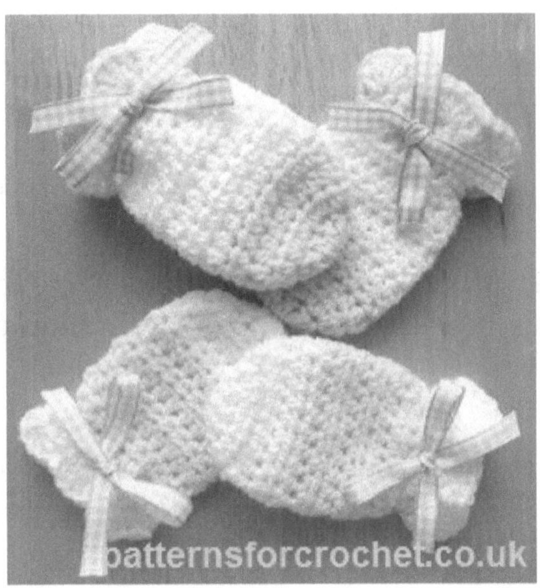

Materials

These mittens are made to fit newborns to size 3

- ¾ Ounce of light-weight yarn

- Crochet hook F/5

- Yarn needle

Directions

1. **Round 1-** Chain 2. Crochet 6 singles crochet stitches in second chain. Place marker in the last stitch. You will have 6 stitches.

2. **Round 2-** Crochet 2 single crochet stitches in each stitch. You will have 12 stitches. Move marker.

3. **Round 3-** *Crochet two single crochet stitches in next two stitches. Two single crochets in next stitch.* Repeat   this pattern for the round. You will have 20 stitches.

4. Repeat round 3 until you have 15 rounds with 20 stitches in each round. You work should measure 3 ¼ inches.

5. **Round 16-** *Single crochet, chain 1, skip 1.* Repeat this pattern for the round. Slip stitch in the 1st single crochet.

6. **Round 17-** Chain 2. Double crochet in each stitch and chain 1 space. Join with a slip stitch to first double crochet. You should have 20 stitches.

7. **Round 18-** Chain 1, crochet 1 single chain in each stitch. Join to first single chains with a slip stitch. Finish off.

Mitten Ties

1. Chain 55. Weave tie through eyelet stitches in round 16. Tie bow at the top of the mitten.

16. Tunisian Stitch Baby Bib

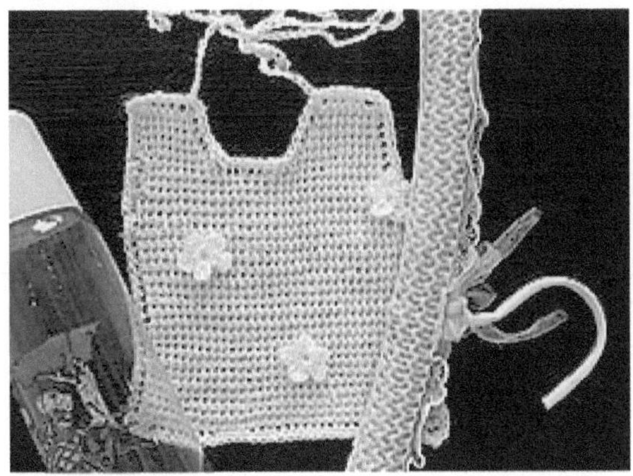

Materials

- 2 balls of 3-ply synthetic baby yarn in two colors of your choice

- 3.5 mm Afghan crochet hook

Directions

1. Chain 36 in color A.

2. **Row 1-25-** Crochet in Tunisian crochet stitch.

3. **Row 26-** Crochet the first 12 stitches, decrease 1 stitch every second row. Do this three times.

4. On the third row decrease, also decrease one stitch on the outside edge.

5. Continue working, skipping 10 stitches in the middle of the row to form an opening for the neck.

6. Crochet to desired length.

Bib Ties

1. Crochet two 8-inch lengths of chain and stitch to each side of the neck opening.

17. Dress It Up Diaper Cover

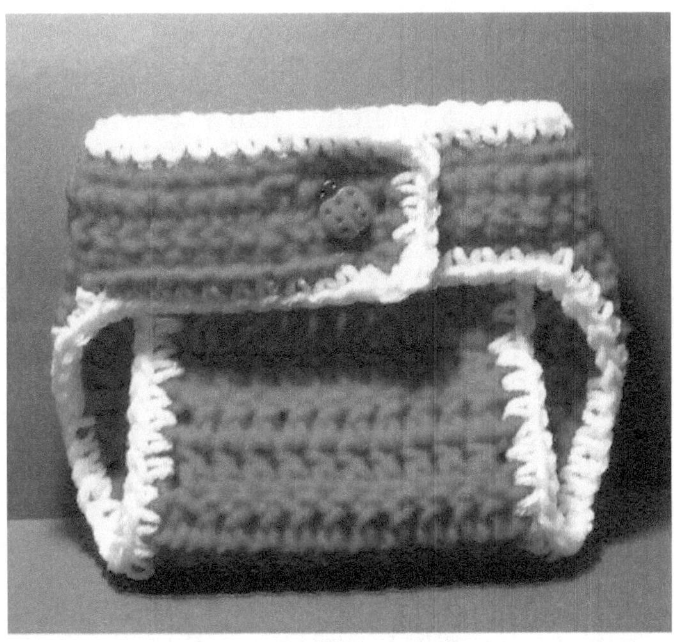

Materials

This diaper cover measures 8 inches wide across the back and 6 inches in length

- 2 Skeins of Soft Worsted Weight Yarn in contrasting colors

- Size H Crochet Hook

- Yarn Needle

- 1 Medium Button

Directions

1. Chain 55. **Row 1-** With main color, single crochet in 2nd chain and in each stitch across. Chain 3 and turn. You will have 54 stitches. **Row 2-** Triple crochet in each stitch across. Chain 1. Turn. You will have 54 stitches. **Row 3-** Single crochet in each stitch across. Fasten off. Weave in ends.

2. **Row 4-** Count 16 stitches from the right of row 3. Slip stitch yarn. Chain 3. Double crochet in next 24 stitches. Chain 1 and turn. You will have 24 stitches. **Row 5-** Single crochet in each stitch across. Chain 3 and Turn. You will have 24 stitches. **Row 6-** Double crochet in each stitch. Chain 1 and turn. You will have 24 stitches. **Row 7-** Single crochet in each stitch. Chain 3 and turn. You will have 24 stitches.

3. **Row 8-** Double crochet in each stitch. Chain 1 and turn. You will have 24 stitches. **Row 9-** Single crochet in each stitch. Chain 3 and turn. You will have 24 stitches. **Row 10-** Decrease double crochet at beginning and end of each row. Double crochet 20 stitches. Chain 1 and turn. You will have 22 stitches.

4. **Row 11-** Single crochet decrease, single crochet next 18 stitches, single crochet decrease. Chain 3 and turn. You will have 20 stitches. **Row 12-** Decrease double crochet, double crochet in next 16 stitches. Double crochet. Chain 1. Turn. You will have 18 stitches. **Row 13-** Single crochet decrease,

single crochet in next 14 stitches, decrease. Chain 3. Turn. You will have 16 stitches.

5. **Row 14**- Double crochet decrease, double crochet in next 12 stitches, decrease double crochet. Chain 1. Turn. You will have 14 stitches. **Row 15**- Single chain in each stitch in the row. Chain 3. Turn. You will have 14 stitches. **Row 16**- Double crochet in each stitch in the row. Chain 1. Turn. You will have 14 stitches.

6. **Row 17**- Single crochet in each stitch in the row. Chain 3. Turn. You will have 14 stitches. **Row 18**- Double crochet in each stitch in the row. Chain 1. Turn. You will have 14 stitches. **Row 19**- Single crochet in each stitch in the row. Chain 3. Turn. You will have 14 stitches.

7. **Row 20**- Double crochet in each stitch in the row. Chain 1. Turn. You will have 14 stitches. **Row 21**- Single crochet in each stitch in the row. Chain 3. Turn. You will have 14 stitches. **Row 22**- Crochet 2 double crochets in first stitch, double crochet in each stitch in the row. Chain 1. Turn. You will have 15 stitches.

8. **Row 23**- Crochet 2 single crochets into first stitch, single crochet into each stitch across. Chain 3. Turn. You will have 16 stitches. **Row 24**- Crochet double crochet in each stitch in the row. Chain 1. Turn. You will have 16 stitches.

9. **Row 25-** Single crochet into each stitch across. Chain 3. Turn. You will have 16 stitches. **Row 26-** Double crochet in each stitch in the row. Chain 3. Turn. You will have 16 stitches. Fasten off and weave in ends.

Edging

1. Single crochet around all the edges of the diaper cover with the contrasting color of yarn. Fasten off.

2. Button holes will be in row 2 in the front. Sew button.

18. Baby Booties

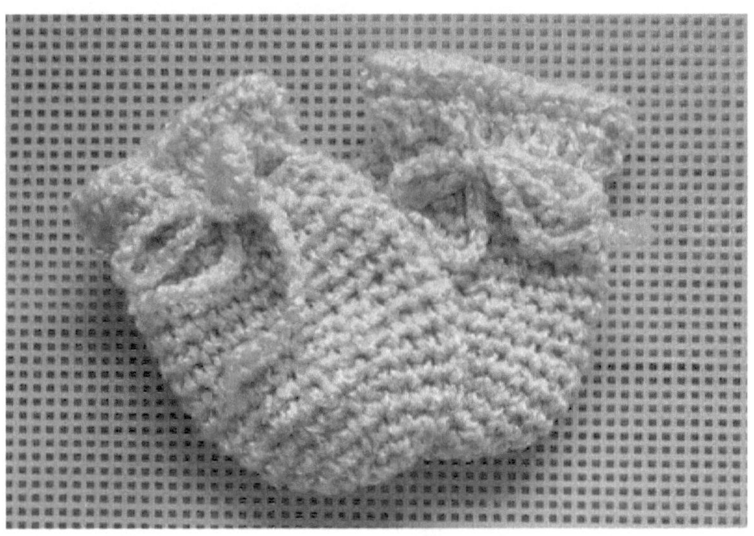

Materials

These booties are 6-month size

- Medium weight soft yarn, in 1 or 2 colors

- Crochet Hook G/6; 4.0

Directions

1. Chain 10. **Round 1**— Start in the second chain and single crochet in next 7 chains. Crochet 5 single crochets in last chain. This is the toe. Working in loops on the back side of the chain, single crochet the next 7 chains. This is the heel. Join with slip stitch to 1st single crochet.

2. **Round 2**— Chain 2. Half double crochet in each of the next 5 stitches. Half double crochet in each of the next 7 single crochets. Crochet 2 half double crochets in each of the last 2 single chains. Join with slip stitch to the top of first chain. Chain 2.

3. **Round 3**— Half-double crochet in same stitch and in each of the next 12 stitches. Crochet 2 half-double crochets in each of the next 3 stitches. Crochet 1 half-double crochet in each of the next 12 stitches. Crochet 2 half double crochets in each of the last 2 stitches.

4. **Round 4**—If you would like a different color on the upper part of the shoe, you can change yarn now. Single crochet 1 stitch in the back of the loop and single crochet in the back loops around the entire sole of the shoe. Slip stitch to beginning stitch.

5. **Round 5**— Chain 1. Single crochet into the stitch and then single crochet into every stitch around the shoe. Slip stitch to first single crochet.

6. **Round 6**— Chain 2. Half-double crochet in the next 9 stitches. Half-double crochet 2 times in the next six stitches. Half double chain around. Slip stitch to top of first chain.

7. **Round 7**— You can switch back to original yarn color if you choose. Chain 1. Single crochet in the same stitch and in each of the next 9 stitches. Single crochet 2 stitches together. Single crochet next stitch. Single crochet next 2 stitches together.

Single crochet around. Join with a slip stitch to the top of the single crochet.

Shoe Tie

1. Chain 5. Single crochet each side of the chain. Find the center of the toe and count four stitches on each side toward the heel. Stitch one end of shoe tie with a slip stitch. Finish. Weave in end. Attach opposite side of shoe tie with yarn and needle.

19. Happy Face Rattle

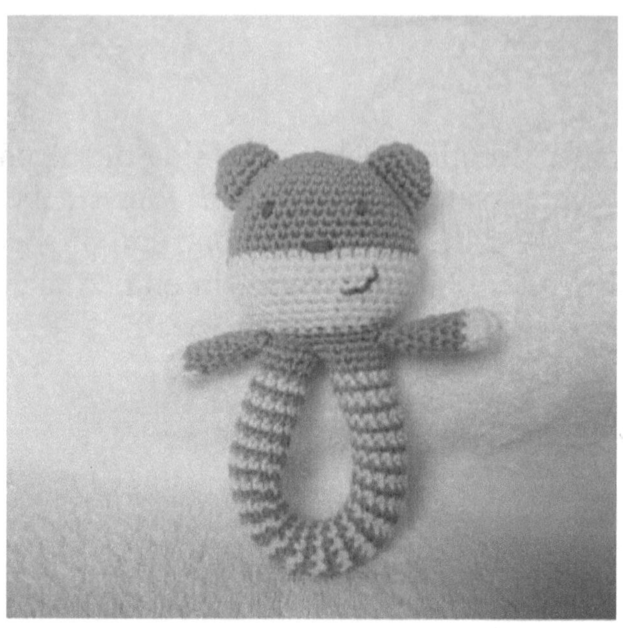

Materials

- Light yarn in two contrasting colors

- Crochet hook H/8; 3.0

- Rattle insert (available on line)

- Embroidery thread

- Stuffing

Directions

Ears, make 2

1. Use yarn color A if you would like the ears the same color as the head. Use color B if you would like contrasting ears. Chain 3. Join. **Round 1**— Crochet 6 single crochets into the ring.

2. **Round 2**— Crochet 2 single crochets into each stitch in the round. You will have 12 stitches.

3. **Round 3,4**—Crochet 1 single crochet into each stitch in the round. You will have 12 stitches.

4. **Round 5**- Single crochet 2 stitches together, repeat to the end. You will have 8 stitches.

5. **Round 6**- Single crochet 2 stitches together, repeat to the end. You will have 4 stitches. Finish off. Leave a long length of yarn to sew each ear to the head.

Arms, make 2

1. In Color B, Chain 3. Join. **Round 1**—Crochet 8 single crochet stitches into the ring.

2. **Round 2**—Crochet 8 single crochet stitches into each stitch in the round.

3. **Round 3-10**—Continue the pattern of round 2. Finish off. Leave a long length of yarn to attach arms.

The Round Head

1. Use yarn color A. Chain 3, slip stitch to form ring. **Round 1**— Crochet 2 single crochets into each chain. **Round 2**— Crochet 2 single crochets into each stitch. You will have 12 stitches. **Round 3**— Crochet *2 single crochets in next stitch, then 1 single crochet*, continue this pattern in the round. You will have 18 stitches.

2. **Round 4**— Crochet *2 single crochets in next stitch, then 2 single crochets*, repeat this pattern in the round. You will have 24 stitches. **Round 5**— Crochet *2 single crochets in next stitch, then 3 single crochets*, repeat this pattern in the round. You will have 30 stitches. **Round 6**— Crochet *2 single crochets in next stitch, then 4 single crochets*, repeat this pattern in the round. You will have 36 stitches.

3. **Round 7-9**— Crochet single chain in each stitch. You will have 36 stitches. **Round 10**— Crochet 2 single crochets in next stitch. Do this three times. Single crochet in next stitch for the next 15 stitches. Crochet 2 single crochet in next stitch, 3 times. Single crochet in next stitch for 15 stitches. You will have 42 stitches

4. **Round 11-13**— Single crochet in each stitch around. You will have 42 stitches. **Round 14-16** – Single crochet in each stitch around. You will have 42 stitches. **Round 17**— Crochet 1 single crochet in the next five stitches. Single crochet 2 stitches

together. Repeat the round. You will now have 36 stitches.

5. **Round 18**— Single crochet the round. You will have 36 stitches. While the head is easily accessible, embroider big eyes, a nose and smiling mouth. The eyes will be placed about round 9. The nose on round 12. Attach the ears at each side of the head on row 5.

6. **Round 19**— *Crochet 1 single crochet in the next 4 stitches, single chain 2 stitches together,* continue this pattern for the round. You will have 30 stitches. **Round 20**— Single crochet the round. You will have 30 stitches.

7. **Round 21**— *Crochet 1 single crochet in next 3 stitches, single chain 2 stitches together,* continue this pattern for the round. You will have 24 stitches. **Round 22**— Single crochet the round. You will have 24 stitches. **Round 23**- Attach arms at the base of the large head by crocheting though both thicknesses. Single crochet the round.

The Handle

1. **Round 24**- Single crochet until you reach the center of the head. Skip 12 stitches. You will work only in the 2nd 12 stitches.

2. **Round 25**- to finish. You will single crochet each stitch in the round. You can change yarn as you like,

not cutting yarn. You will be working in a spiral.
The spiral should be 7-12 inches long.

Finishing

1. Stuff the rattle carefully into the head. Attach the end of the spiral to the open 12 stitches at the base of the head. This will form a ring.

2. Test to make sure the ring is firmly attached. Finish off. Weave in ends.

20. Diaper Wipes Wallet

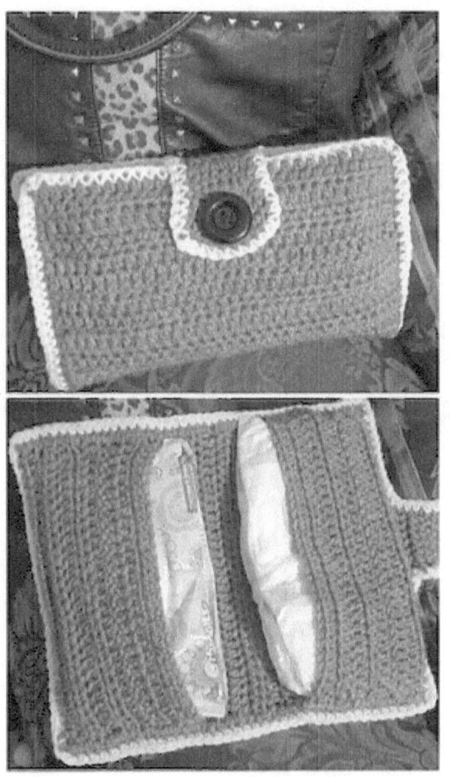

Materials

- Worsted weight 10 ply yarn

- Crochet hook

- Button

- Matching thread

Directions

Wallet

1. Chain 29. **Row 1**— Half double crochet in 3rd chain and continue the row. Chain 2 and turn.

2. **Row 2**— Half double crochet the row. Turn.

3. **Row 3**— Chain 3. Double crochet the row. Turn.

4. **Row 4-41**— Continue alternating Row 2 and Row 3. Fasten off.

5. With 9 rows in the middle, fold each end to the center. Single crochet along each side to create pockets. They should be nine rows deep. Fasten off.

Strap

1. Attach yarn to the bottom of one of the pocket, 9 stitches from the outside edge.

2. Chain 3. Double crochet in next 8 stitches.

3. Chain 3 and double crochet two more rows. Chain 2 and single chain the stitches.

Button Hole

1. Chain 2, single crochet the next 2 stitches, chain 3, and then single crochet the last 3 stitches.

2. Chain 2 and single crochet the next 2 stitches, single crochet the next 3 stiches, single crochet the next 3 stitches.

3. Chain 2. Half double chain the row. Fasten off. Sew button on wallet opposite the button hole.

Finishing

1. Single crochet all edges of the wallet, including strap. You can use the same color or contrasting yarn.

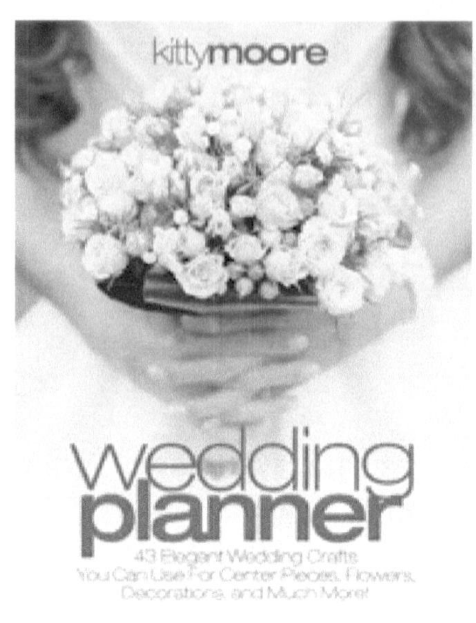

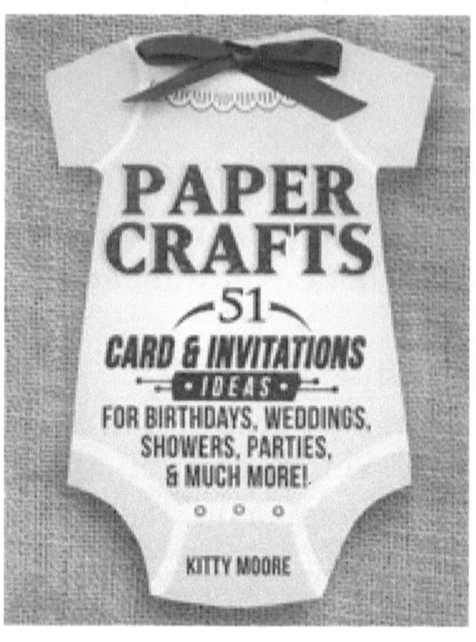

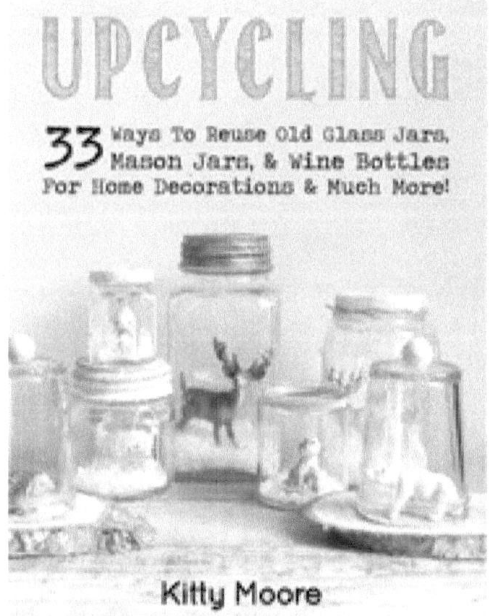

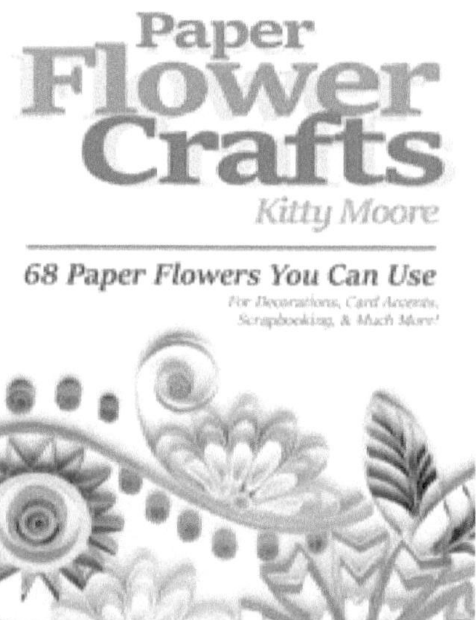

Check out Kitty's books at:

ArtsCraftsAndMore.com/go/books

21. Baby Wash Cloth

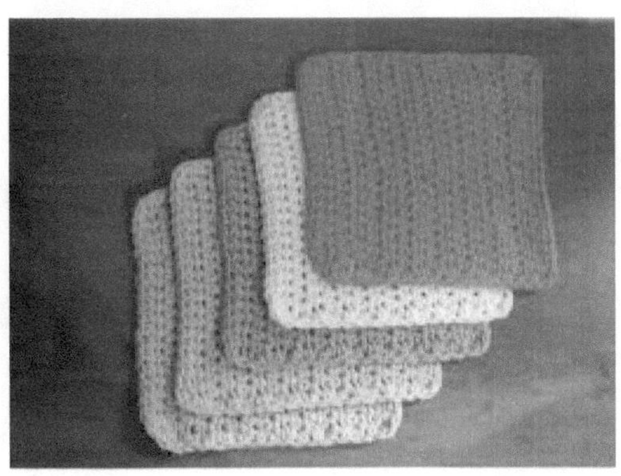

Materials

- Sport weight crochet cotton

- Steel Hook – B/1; 2.25

Directions

1. **Row 1**— Chain 40. Single crochet in 2nd chain from hook and each chain to the end. Chain 3 and turn. You will have 39 stitches.

2. **Row 2**— Skip 1st stitch. *Half double crochet in next stitch. Chain one. Skip next stitch, half double crochet.* Repeat this pattern the rest of the row. Chain 1 and turn.

3. **Row 3**— Single crochet in same stitch as begging chain 1. Single crochet in each chain 1 space and in each half double crochet across. Chain 1 and turn.

4. **Row 4-33**—Repeat rows 2 and 3.

5. **Row 34**- Repeat row 2.

6. **Row 35**— Single crochet in same stitch as beginning chain 1. Single crochet in each chain 1 space and in each half double crochet. Chain 3. Do not turn

Edging

1. In the large holes at the edge of the wash cloth, follow this pattern around the entire washcloth, *4 double crochets in the corner space, single crochet in the next space, 5 double crochets in the next space, single crochet in the next space.*

2. Join with a slip stitch. Fasten off and weave in ends.

22. Baby Aviator Hat with Goggles

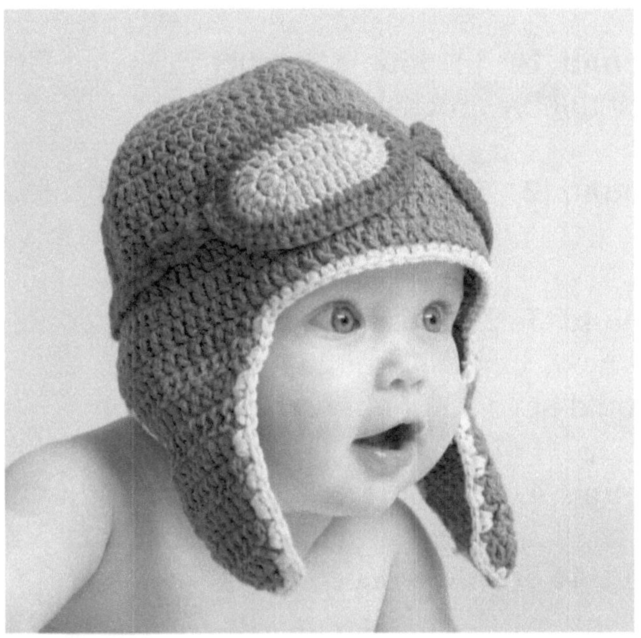

Materials

- Any worsted weight yarn in brown and gray

- Bulky weight yarn in white or off white

- Crochet Hook Size H

- Tapestry needle for edging and finishing

Directions

This pattern is for 0-3-month-old babies but the size can be adjusted for older kids.

1. Start by making a magic ring, this part of the pattern will be worked in the round.

2. **Round 1-** 11 double crochet in magic ring, join to first double crochet, chain 2.

3. **Round 2-** 2 double crochet in each around, join, chain 2. You should end up with 22 double crochet.

4. **Round 3-** 2 double crochet in first, double crochet in next, repeat around, join, chain 2. Now you should have 33 double crochet.

5. **Round 4-** 2 double crochet in first, double crochet in next 2, repeat around, join, chain 2. You should have 44 double crochet.

6. **Round 5-10-** Double crochet in each around, join, chain 2. There should still be 44 double crochet because you did not increase in that round. Do not finish off just leave the string for now you will use it later to attach the earflaps.

Earflaps (Make 2)

1. Chain 1, single crochet in next 10, chain 1, turn.

2. **Row 2-** Single crochet decrease, single crochet in next 6, single crochet decrease, chain 1, turn.

3. **Row 3-** Single crochet across. You should have 8 single crochet.

4. **Row 4-** Single crochet decrease, single crochet in next 4, single crochet decrease, chain 1, turn.

5. **Row 5-** SC across. You should have 6 SC.

6. **Row 6-** SC decrease, SC in next 2, SC decrease, chain 1, turn.

7. **Row 7-** SC across. You should have 4 SC. Attach earflaps to the hat on either side.

Aviator Goggles

1. Use the gray worsted yarn to make the aviator goggles for the front of the hat. Chain 5, 2 single crochet in second chain from hook, single crochet in next 2 stitches, 2 single crochet in last stitch, chain 1, turn. Row 2- Single crochet in each stitch, chain 1, turn.

2. Row 3- 2 single crochet in first stitch, single crochet in next 4, 2 single crochet in last, chain 1, turn. Row 4-8- Single crochet in each stitch, chain 1, turn. Row 9- Single crochet decrease, single crochet in next 4; single crochet decrease, chain 1, turn. Row 10- Single crochet in each stitch, chain 1 turn.

3. Row 11- Single crochet decrease, single crochet in next 4, chain 1, turn. Row 12- Single crochet in each stitch, chain 1, turn. Row 13- 2 single crochet in first stitch, single crochet in next 4, chain 1, turn. Row 14- Single crochet in each stitch, chain 1, turn.

4. Row 15- 2 single crochet in first, single crochet in next 4, 2 single crochet in last stitch, chain 1, turn. Row 16-20- Single crochet in each stitch, chain 1, turn. Row 21- Single crochet decrease, single crochet in next 4, single crochet decrease, chain 1, turn.

5. Row 22- Single crochet in each stitch, chain 1, turn. Row 23- Single crochet decrease, single crochet in next 2, single crochet decrease, chain 1, fasten off weave in ends. Crochet around the entire goggle form with the bulky white yarn using single crochet.

6. Use the bulky white yarn to create eye holes in the goggles by slip stitching a circle on either side of the goggles with the white bulky yarn. Use the tapestry needle to surface sew the goggles onto the front of the hat. Edge the entire hat with 1-2 rows of single crochet in the white bulky yarn.

23. Dragon Scale Baby Booties

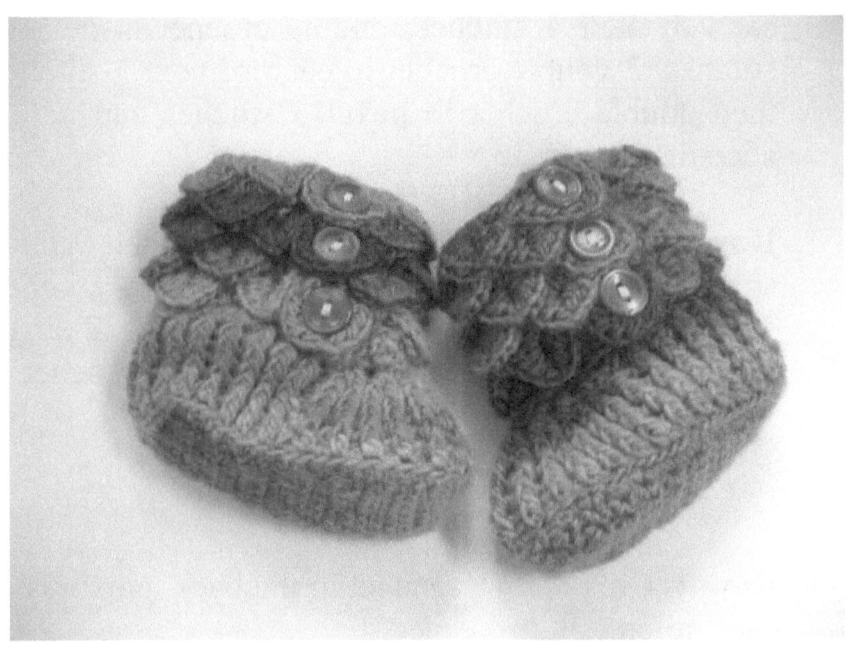

Materials

- Worsted weight yarn in any color and a 3.5mm crochet hook

Directions

Sole

1. Chain 17. **Row 1-** 4 double crochet in 3rd chain from hook. Double crochet in the next 13 stiches. Work 5 double crochet stitches in last stitch, turn, then double crochet in the next 13 stitches, finish with a slip stitch.

2. **Row 2-** The Ch2 counts as a double crochet, then double crochet in same space. 2 double crochet in each of next 4 stitches, double crochet in next 13 stitches, 2 double crochet in each of next 5 stitches, then double crochet in next 13 stitches and with a slip stitch.

3. **Row 3-** For this row Ch1= 1 single crochet. Work 2 single crochet stitches in each of next 8 stitches. Then single crochet in the next 15 stitches. 2 single crochet in each of next 8 stitches, single crochet in next 14 stitches, and end with a slip stitch.

Boot

1. **Row 4-** Ch2, double crochet in the back loop only of each stitch.

2. **Row 5-** Ch2, work in the front loop of the double crochet in next stitch, then work in the back loop of the double crochet in the next stitch, then again, the front loop of the double crochet up to the end. The last stitch should always be in the front loop of the double crochet.

3. **Row 6-** At this point you have to find 2 front loop double crochet stitches from the middle of the top toe to start decreasing, then count 6 front loop double crochet to the left and 6 front loop double crochet to the right. You should have a grand total of 14 front loop double crochet stitches. Mark the stitches with a stitch marker or a small piece of yarn.

4. Ch2 and continue working the front loop double crochet, then the back loop double crochet up to the first marked front loop double crochet. In order to start decreasing, work the front loop double crochet and the back look double crochet together in a double crochet.

5. Keep doing this stitch set through the 13-front loop double crochet up to the last mark, then continue with front loop double crochet and back loop double crochet together in one double crochet. End with a slip stitch.

6. **Row 7-** Ch2, front loop double crochet and back loop double crochet alternately up to the first decreased stitch from last row. Double crochet the front loop and back loop together for the next 7 stitches. Then continue to alternate front loop double crochet and back loop double crochet until the end. Finish with a slip stitch.

7. **Row 8-** Ch2, alternate front loop and back loop double crochet up to top toe decreasing stitches. There are 7 decreased double crochet from last row so in those stitches work: double crochet 2 stitches together, double crochet 3 stitches together, double crochet 2 stitches together until the end. Continue with the front loop then back loop double crochet, then end with a slip stitch. If you want to change colors and make the dragon scales different colors this is where you change colors.

Dragon Scales

1. **Row 9**- Ch 2 and double crochet in same stitch. Ch2, skip 2 stitches, 2 double crochet in 3rd stitch, ch2, skip 2 stitches. 2 double crochet in 3rd stitch. Do this all around. Ch2 and slip stitch at the end.

2. **Row 10**- Ch2 in the first double crochet, work 4 double crochet around the first double crochet. Then chain 1, turn your work, and work 5 double crochet around the second double crochet from last row. Single crochet in next set of two double crochet. Work 5 double crochet around the first double crochet ch1 space, turn and do 5 double crochet around the second double crochet. Single crochet in next set of two double crochet. Keep doing this until you work all the sets of 2 double crochet, the last one has to be single crochet. Slip stitch in ch2 stitches from first shell.

3. **Row 11**- Work slip stitches up to the center of the same set of scales. Ch2 and make a double crochet in the center of scales. Ch 2 then work 2 double crochet in the single crochet stitch, Ch2 and work 2 double crochet in the center of the second dragon scale. Ch2 and 2 double crochet in next single crochet stitch from last row. Continue this until you finish the base for the next dragon scale stitch row. Ch2 and slip stitch in the ch2 stitch.

4. **Row 12**- Start the row with a single crochet in the first scale space, then go to next scale space and work 5 double crochet around first double crochet,

ch1, 5 double crochet around the second double crochet. Single crochet in the next space, 5 double crochet around first double crochet. Keep working this pattern until the size is right. Finish in a single crochet and a slip stitch.

5. Keep repeating R12 until you have a total of 5 dragon scale stitch rows, fasten off. To finish the boot work around in reverse crochet stitch through the loops that are left.

24. Textured Block Baby Blanket

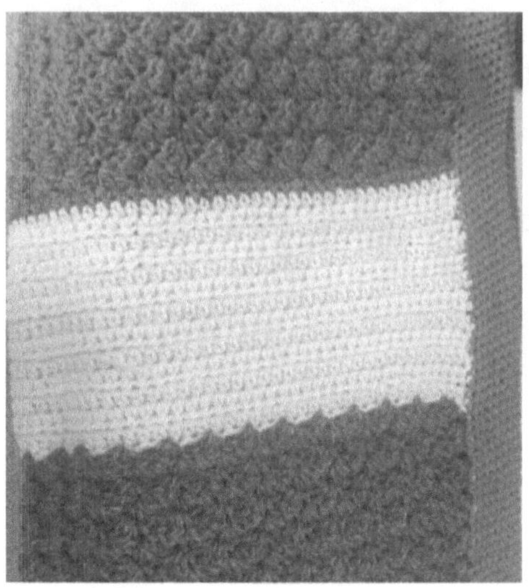

Materials

- Worsted weight yarn in colors of your choice

- Size H crochet hook or size needed for gauge

- Tapestry needle to sew the blocks together

Directions

This blanket is made of textured squares that are sewn together, so you can make it in any size that you want. There are two styles of blocks and you can sew them together in any color or pattern arrangement that you like. Babies like colors and textures so you can make lots of different patterns by making these two textured blocks in lots of different colors and combining them.

Block one

1. Ch12. **Row 1-** 12 Single crochet to the end of the row, chain 1, turn and continue single crocheting.

2. **Edging-** chain 3, then single crochet around all 4 edges of the block. Work 3 single crochet in each corner to maintain the square shape. Fasten off.

Block Two

1. Ch12.

2. **Rows 1-**12 double crochet in the front loop of each stitch only. Continue to the end of the row, chain 1, turn and continue double crochet in the front loop only. This will create a ridged texture.

3. **Edging-** chain 3, then single crochet around the entire block working 2 single crochet in each corner. Fasten off.

4. Make as many squares as you need to make the blanket the size you want. Sew the blocks together in alternating directions with different textures joined together.

5. **Blanket edging-** In whatever color you choose work 10-20 rows of single crochet around the entire blanket, always working 3 single crochet in each corner.

25. Swaddle Sack

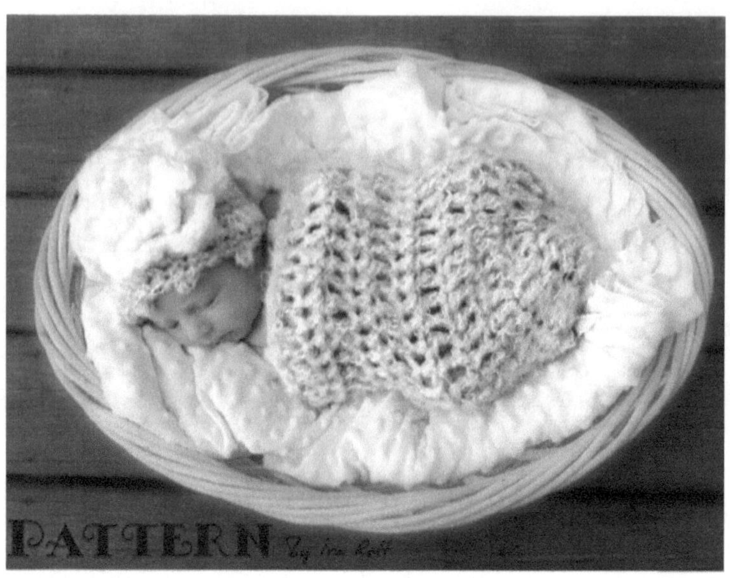

Materials

Heavy worsted weight yarn or bulky yarn. Don't use wool yarn for baby items because some babies are allergic to wool. Cotton yarn is a great choice. These swaddle sacks are great photo props for newborns

This is a simple pattern that you can really make unique by using different colors of yarn for stripes and other patterns.

- 6mm crochet hook

- Yarn needle for weaving in ends

Directions

To make the sack

1. **Round 1**- Ch 2, make 9 half double crochet in the 2nd chain from hook, slip stitch to join in first half double crochet stitch. **Round 2**- Ch 1, work 2 half double crochet in each stitch around, join with a slip stitch. **Round 3**- Ch 1, half double crochet in first stitch, 2 half double crochet in next stitch repeat around, join with a slip stitch.

2. **Round 4**- Ch 1, half double crochet in first 2 stitches, work 2 half double crochet in next stitch repeat around, join with a slip stitch. **Round 5**- Ch 1, half double crochet in first 3 stitches, work 2 half double crochet in next stitch repeat around, join with a slip stitch. **Round 6**- Ch 1, half double crochet in first 8 stitches, work 2 half double crochet in next stitch repeat around, join with a slip stitch.

3. **Round 7**- Ch 1, skip first stitch, half double crochet around until 1 stitch remains, work 2 half double crochet in last stitch, join in first half double crochet with a slip stitch. **Round 8**- Ch 1, half double crochet in each stitch around, join with a slip stitch.

4. **Round 9-25**- Repeat Round 7 and Round 8. **Round 26**- Ch 1, back loop only half double crochet in first stitch, front loop only half double crochet in next stitch repeat between to end, join with a slip stitch. **Round 27-29**- Repeat Round 26. Fasten off and weave in ends.

26. 2 Hour Baby Afghan

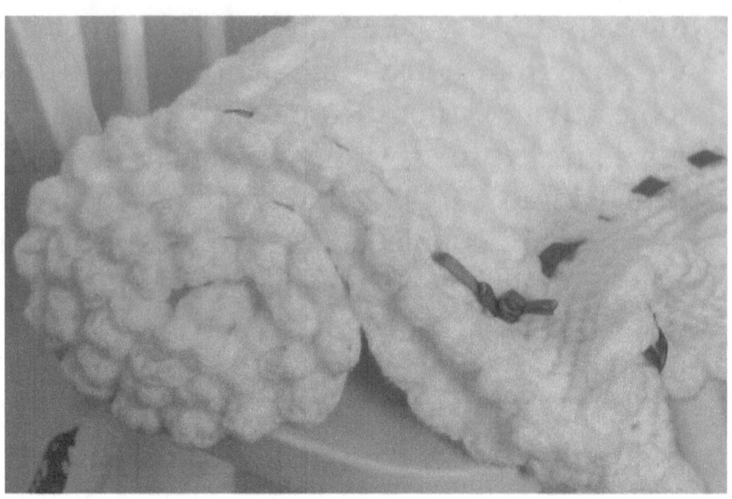

Materials

- Worsted weight yarn in any color or colors that you want. Use two strands of the yarn held together to make the blanket thick. This is an easy pattern to do in stripes if you want to make it more colorful

- Hook size- M/N or 9mm

Directions

Bubble Stitch- 1 single crochet and 2 double crochet stitches all in the same stitch.

1. Chain 62.

2. **Row 1-** Bubble stitch in second chain stitch from the hook. Skip two chains and continue bubble stitch all

the way across. When you get to the last stitch just work 1 single crochet in that stitch, chain 2 and turn.

3. **Row 2**- Work 2 double crochet stitches in the single crochet that ended the previous row. Bubble stitch across. Chain 2 then turn and repeat Row 2 until the blanket is the size you want. Fasten off and weave in the ends. This blanket doesn't need any edging or trim.

27. Thick and Cozy Stroller Blanket

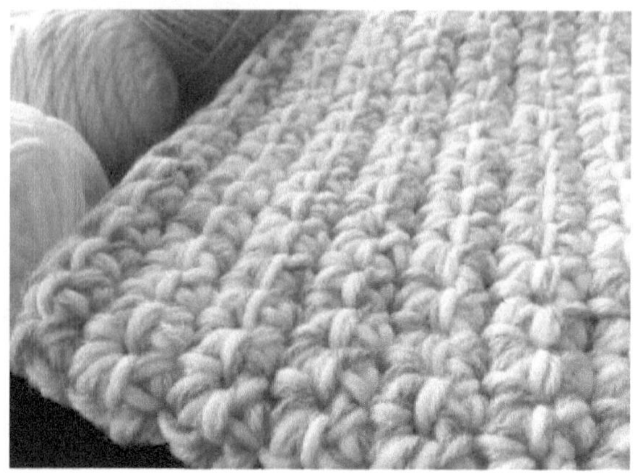

Materials

- Worsted weight yarn in any colors that you like

- Crochet hook Size G or 4mm

- Tapestry needle for weaving in the ends

Directions

Dual Single Crochet Stitch- This stitch is really just 2 single crochet stitches worked together. To make this stitch insert your hook into a stitch and draw up a loop. Insert the hook into the next stitch and draw up a loop. Yarn over and draw the hook through all three loops that are on the hook. That is a Dual Single Crochet stitch and it will make the ripple pattern in the blanket.

1. Ch 132.

2. **Row 1-** Work 2 single crochet in 2nd ch from hook, single crochet in next 2 ch. Work a Dual Single Crochet Stitch twice, single crochet in next 2 ch, 2 single crochet in each of next 2 ch, single crochet in next 2 ch. Repeat this until you get to the last 7 ch. Then work 2 Dual Single Crochet stitches, single crochet in the next 2 ch, and single crochet in the last ch. Turn. There should be 13 ripples in the row when you are done.

3. **Row 2-** Ch 1, turn, 2 single crochet in first st, single crochet in next 2 sts. From there Dual Single Crochet stitch twice, single crochet in next 2 sts, 2 single crochet in each of next 2 sts, single crochet in next 2 sts; repeat until the last 7 sts. Then Dual Single Crochet stitch twice, single crochet in the next 2 stitches, and work 2 single crochet in the stitch in the row. Turn. Repeat Row 2 until the blanket is the size you want. Weave in ends to finish. This blanket doesn't need edging.

28. Cozy Baby Sling

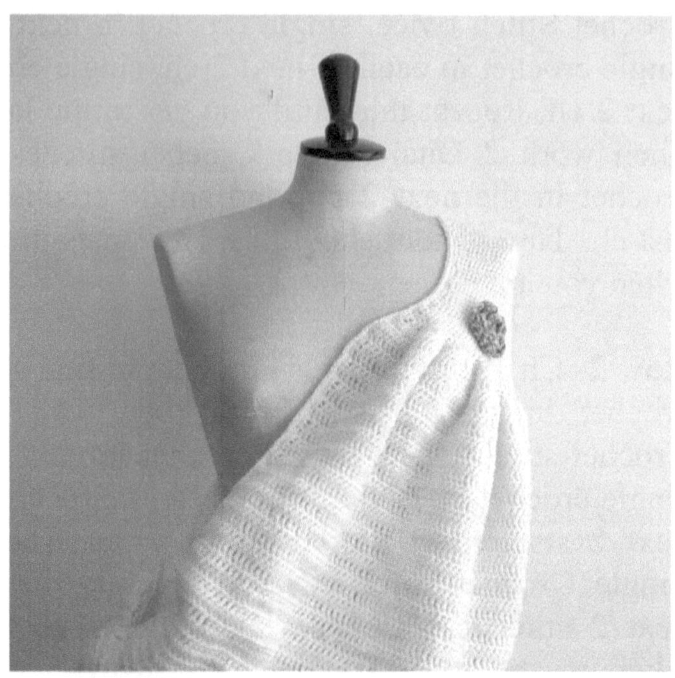

Materials

- Worsted weight yarn in any colors that you want to use

- Crochet hook size H

- Tapestry needle for weaving in the ends

Directions

1. Start the sling by chaining 6, then joining the ends together with a slip stitch to make a ring.

2. **Round 1-** Chain 3 and work six double crochet stitches into the space inside the ring that you started with.

3. **Round 2-** Chain 3 and work six double crochet stitches into the ring that you just made. Chain 1 and work 2 more double crochet stitches. Chain 3 and continue working in the round, putting a double crochet stitch into each chain-1 space and chaining 1. Continue working like this adding one increase per row until the sling part is big enough for an infant.

Strap

1. When the sling part is the right size switch from rounds to rows. Start with one decrease per row and keep going, adding in an additional decrease wherever you need to in order to make the strap the right width to fit comfortably. Keep going until the strap is long enough. Then fasten off. Use the needle to sew the strap to the edge of the sling.

2. Weave in all the ends and you're done.

29. Quick Baby Bib

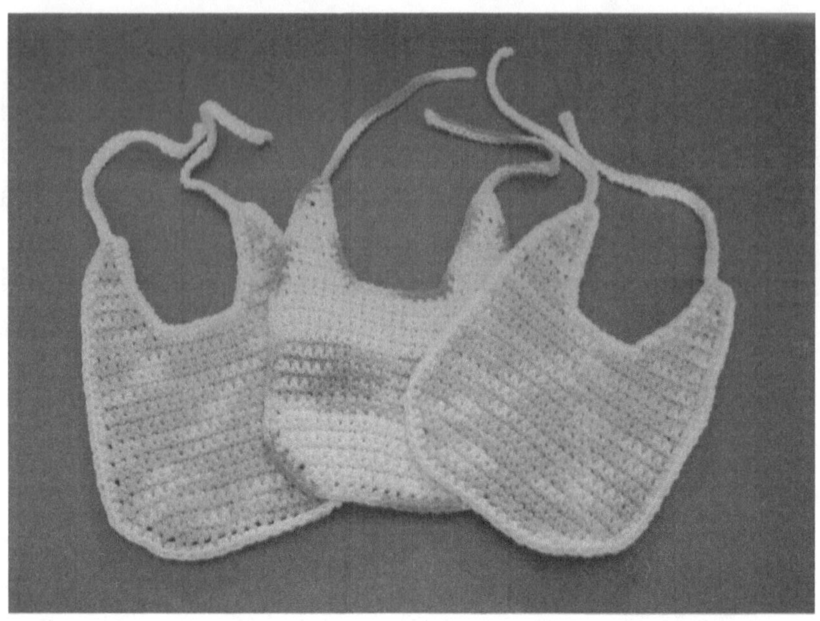

Materials

- Medium weight cotton yarn in any color. Try a variegated yarn to make it more colorful

- Crochet hook size I or 5.50mm

Directions

Half Double Crochet: To make a Half Double Crochet stitch yarn over like you would for a double crochet but instead of pulling only one loop through pull all three loops on the hook through and finish the stitch. It's like a single crochet except you have three loops on the hook.

1. **Round 1-** Ch 3, 8 half double crochet stitches in third ch from hook. Slip stitch in top of beginning ch-3.

2. **Round 2-** Ch 2, turn, 2 half double crochet in each half double crochet around, sl st in top of beginning ch-2.

3. **Round 3-** Ch 2, turn, 2 half double crochet in next half double crochet, half double crochet in next half double crochet around, sl st in top of beginning ch-2.

4. **Round 4-** Ch 2, turn, 2 half double crochet in next half double crochet, half double crochet in next 2 half double crochet around, slip stitch in top of beginning ch-2.

5. **Round 5-** Ch 2, turn, 2 half double crochet in next half double crochet, half double crochet in next 3 half double crochet around, slip stitch in top of beginning ch-2.

6. **Round 6-** Ch 2, turn, 2 half double crochet in next half double crochet, half double crochet in next 4 half double crochet around, slip stitch in top of beginning ch-2.

7. **Round 7-** Ch 2, turn, 2 half double crochet in next half double crochet, half double crochet in next 5 half double crochet.

8. **Round 8-** Ch 4, turn, 2 triple crochet stitches in next half double crochet, dc in next 2 half double crochet,

half double crochet in next 4 half double crochet, 2 half double crochet in next half double crochet, half double crochet in next 6 half double crochet, 2 half double crochet in next half double crochet, half double crochet in next 2 half double crochet, dc in next 2 half double crochet, triple crochet in next 2 half double crochet.

9. At this point don't finish off or fasten off, you are going to make the straps right on the piece.

First Strap

1. Ch 25 or as long as you want your strap, then finish off.

Second Strap

1. Use a loop to attach your yarn to top of ch-4 at beginning of round 8, ch 25 or as long as you want your strap, then finish off.

30. Cute Flower Pacifier Holders

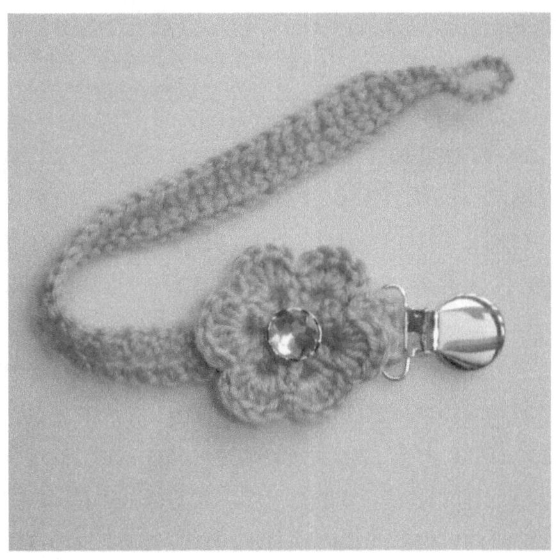

Materials

- Medium weight cotton yarn in any colors but you will need 2 colors

- Crochet hook size F or 3.75 MM

- Tapestry Needle

- Suspender Clip– either 3/4" or 1"

Directions

Strap

1. Using color 1, chain 50.

2. **Row 1-** Half double crochet in 2nd ch from hook and continue working half double crochet stitches down length of chain. In last chain, work 5 half double crochet stitches.

3. **Row 2-** Working on reverse side of chain, continue with half double crochet all the way back to the other end. Finish with a slip stitch in the 1st half double crochet. Fasten off and weave in ends.

4. **Row 3-** Use color 2 and pull up a loop in the center stitch at either end of the strap. Slip stitch into next st if using a 3/4" suspender clip, or single crochet in the next stitch if using a 1" clip, and continue single crochet stitches down the length of the strap.

5. **Row 4-** Chain 25 to create the loop, and then slip stitch and single crochet into next st, and continue single crochet stitches back down the length of the chain. That will complete the border all the way around. Fasten off, leaving a 12-inch piece of yarn for attaching to the clip.

Flower

For the clip end, you can use any applique or flower you like. You can also use this basic pattern for a flower to create a lion, bear or another cute animal.

1. Start with a magic circle. **Round 1-** 12 double crochet stitches around the circle. Join with a slip stitch.

2. **Round 2-** Slip stitch in next stitch. Ch 2. Work 2 double crochet stitches in same st. Then 2 double crochet in next st. Ch 2. Slip st in same st as last double crochet.

3. **Rounds 3-9-** Repeat Round 2 until the flower is how you want or until the animal face is finished if you are making an animal.

To Add the Clip

1. Fold the end without the loop over the clip. Using the tail of yarn that is left on that end use a needle to sew the strap closed around the clip, attaching the clip to the holder strap.

31. Easy Diaper Cover

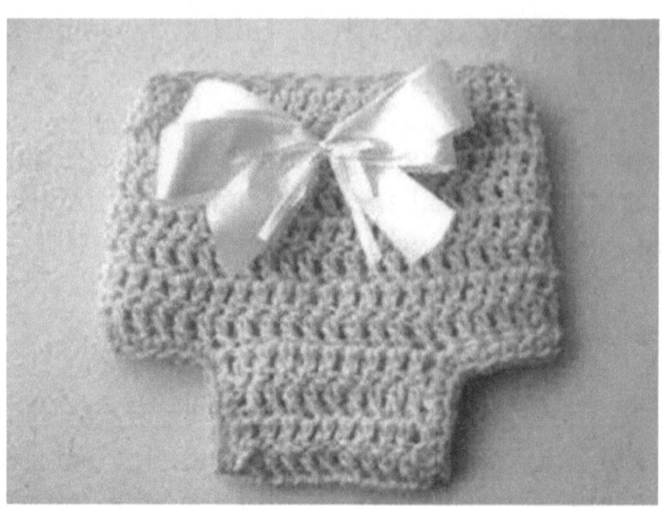

Materials

- Worsted weight yarn in several colors. You will make this cover holding all the strands of yarn together

- Crochet hook size I

- 2 buttons

- Tapestry needle

Directions

1. Start with 12 chains. **Row 1-** Single crochet in 2nd ch from hook and every ch across. Ch1. Turn.

2. **Row 2–12-** Single crochet c in first single crochet, ch 1, skip 1 single crochet, single crochet in next single crochet across.

3. **Row 13-** Ch 1, turn, single crochet in first single crochet, ch 1, single crochet in next 2 single crochet across, single crochet in last single crochet.

4. **Row 14–16-** Ch 1, turn, single crochet in first single crochet, ch 1, skip 1 single crochet, single crochet in next single crochet across.

5. **Row 17-** Ch 1, turn, single crochet in first single crochet, ch 1, single crochet in next 2 across, ch 1, single crochet in last.

6. **Row 18 and 19-** Ch 1, turn, single crochet in first single crochet, ch 1, skip 1 single crochet, single crochet in next single crochet).

Back Piece

1. Chain 40.

2. **Row 1-** Single crochet in 2nd chain from hook and every ch across – 39.

3. **Row 2-** Ch 1, turn, single crochet in first single crochet, ch 1, skip 1 single crochet, single crochet in next across. Sew two pieces together and sew a button on each end.

32. Primary Colors Block Blanket

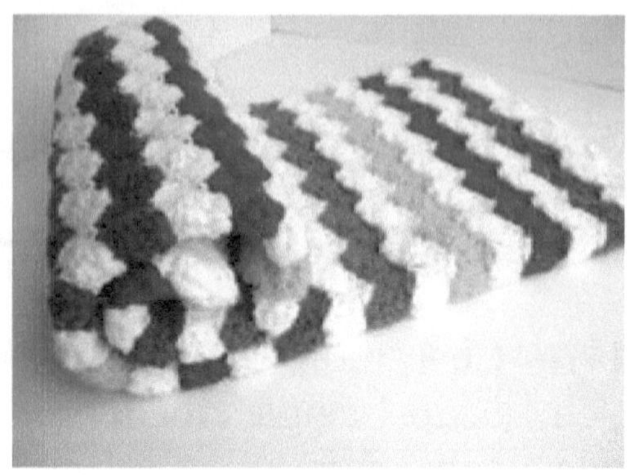

Materials

- Worsted weight yarn in primary colors

- Worsted weight yarn in white

- Crochet hook size I or 5.50mm

Directions

Make one of these strips in each primary color. They will be joined together to make the blanket.

Shell Stich- To make a Shell stitch work 3 double crochet in the chain 2 space.

1. Chain 33.

2. **Row 1**- Single crochet in 2nd Ch from hook, Skip 1 St, Single crochet, Ch 2, Single crochet all in the next St, Skip 2 stitches, single crochet, ch2, single

crochet in the next stitch and repeat all the way across to the last 3 Stitches. Single crochet,ch2,single crochet in next St, Skip 1, Single crochet in the last St.

3. **Row 2-** Ch 3. Turn, work Shell stitches across. Double crochet in last stitch.

4. **Row 3-** Ch 1, Turn, Single crochet in 1st St, Skip 1 St, then again work a single crochet,ch2,single crochet in the next stitch. Continue across.

5. **Rows 4–69-** Repeat Rows 2 and 3.

6. **Row 70-** Repeat Row 2.

Joining

1. To join the strips, make sure the right side of each strip is facing you. With white yarn, single crochet the strips together.

Edging

1. To finish off the blanket go around the entire blanket making single crochet stitches in white yarn. When you get to each corner make 3 single crochet stitches in the corner stitch. Do this for 6-10 rows until the blanket is the size you want.

33. Baby Mittens with a Cord

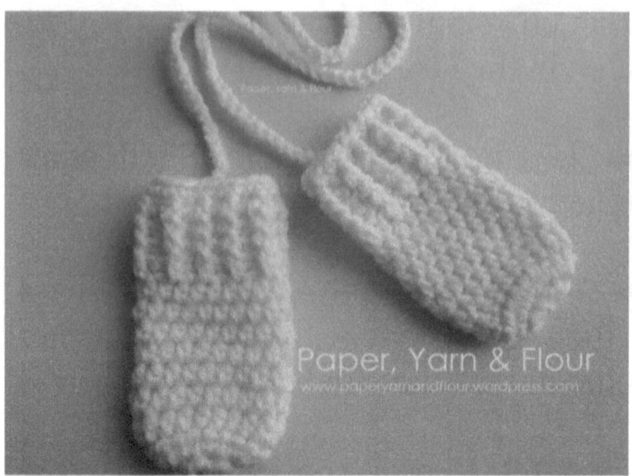

Materials

- Worsted weight yarn in any color

- Crochet hook size H or 4mm

Directions

Make 2

1. Ch4, join with a slip stitch to first ch.

2. **Round 1-** Ch3, work 9double crochet into ring, sl st to top of ch3 on beginning or round. Turn.

3. **Round 2-** Ch2, 1 half double crochet in base of ch2, 2 half double crochet in each double crochet to end, sl st to top of ch2. Turn.

4. **Round 3-10-** Ch2, 1 half double crochet in each half double crochet to end, sl st to top of ch2 on beginning of round. Turn.

5. **Round 11-** Ch1, 1single crochet in base of ch1, ch2, skip 1 half double crochet, 1single crochet in each of next 2 half double crochet, ch2, skip 1half double crochet, repeat around. Turn.

6. **Round 12-** Ch1, 1single crochet in base of ch1, 1single crochet in each ch2 space and single crochet to end, sl st to join. Turn.

7. **Round 13-** Ch1, 1single crochet in base of ch1, skip 1single crochet, 5 double crochet in next single crochet, skip 1single crochet, 1single crochet in next single crochet, repeat to last 3 single crochet, skip 1single crochet, 5 double crochet in next single crochet, skip 1single crochet, sl st to first single crochet on beginning of round.

Cord

1. Chain 100 or however many chains are needed to make the mittens fit the size of the child. Join to the cuff of the other mitten and fasten off.

34. Owl Hat

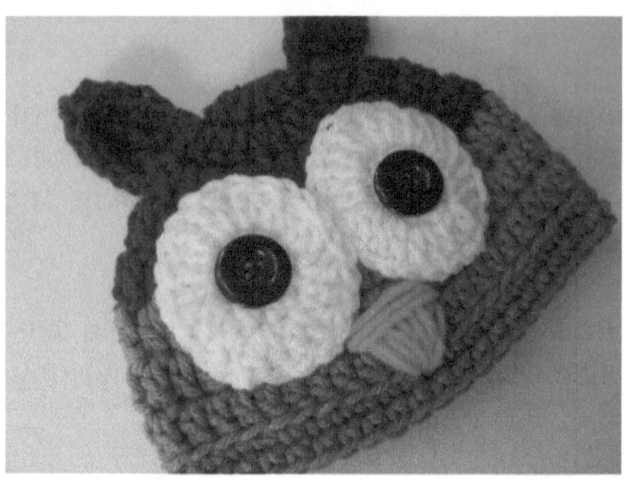

Materials

- Worsted weight yarn in several colors. Choose one for the main color and the others to make the owl's eyes. White is a good choice for the eyed but you can use any colors

- Crochet hook size H or 5mm

- Tapestry needle

- 2 ½ inch or ¾ inch black buttons for the pupils of the eyes

Directions

1. Magic Ring, Ch 2, 9 double crochet in magic ring, join to first double crochet, ch 2.

2. **Round 2-** 2 double crochet in each around, join to first double crochet, ch 2.

3. **Round 3-** 2 double crochet, double crochet in next, repeat around, join, ch 2.

4. **Round 4-** 2 double crochet, double crochet in next 2, repeat around, join, ch 2.

5. **Round 5-** 2 double crochet, double crochet in next 3, repeat around, join, ch 2.

6. **Round 6-** Double crochet around.

7. **Round 7-10-** Double crochet around do not fasten off, begin on first earflap as written below for this size.

Earflap 1

1. **Row 1-** Ch 2, half double crochet 10, chain 2, turn.

2. **Row 2-** Half double crochet decrease, half double crochet in next 6, half double crochet decrease chain 2, turn. **Row 3-** Half double crochet across, chain 2, turn.

3. **Row 4-** Half double crochet decrease, half double crochet in next 4, half double crochet decrease, chain 2, turn.

4. **Row 5-** Half double crochet across, chain 2, turn.

5. **Row 6-** Half double crochet decrease, half double crochet in next 2, half double crochet decrease, chain 2, turn.

6. **Row 7-** 2 half double crochet decreases, chain 2, turn.

7. **Row 8-** Half double crochet decrease, fasten off leaving long tail.

Earflap 2

1. **Row 1-** Chain 2, half double crochet 10, chain 2, turn.

2. **Row 2-** Half double crochet decrease, half double crochet in next 6, half double crochet decrease, chain 2, turn.
3. **Row 3-** Half double crochet across, chain 2, turn.

4. **Row 4-** Half double crochet decrease, half double crochet in next 4, half double crochet decrease, chain 2, turn.

5. **Row 5-** Half double crochet across, chain 2, turn.

6. **Row 6-** Half double crochet decrease, half double crochet in next 2, half double crochet decrease, chain 2, turn.

7. **Row 7-** 2 half double crochet decreases, chain 2, turn.

8. **Row 8-** Half double crochet decrease, chain 1, turn.

9. Continue to single crochet around the entire hat. Join to first single crochet and fasten off, leaving long tail.

Eyes (Make 2)

1. In white make a magic Ring, ch 2.

2. **Round 1-** 10 double crochet in chain, ch 2.

3. **Round 2-** 2 double crochet in same stitch and in each stitch around, join, chain 1.

4. **Round 3-** Single crochet in same stitch, 2 single crochet in next, repeat that pattern around, join to first single crochet, fasten off leaving long tail to sew on.

5. After sewing the eyes to the front of the hat sew a button in the center of each eye to make the pupil.

Nose

1. Chain 6.

2. Slip stitch in 2nd chain from hook, single crochet, half double crochet, double crochet, double crochet, fasten off leaving long tail to sew on. Sew on the nose.

Ears

1. Cut two strands of 12-inch-long pieces of yarn in each color.

2. Loop through 2 double crochets in the crease of the 3rd round.

3. Knot and trim to about 1-inch long.

35. Bootie Knee Socks

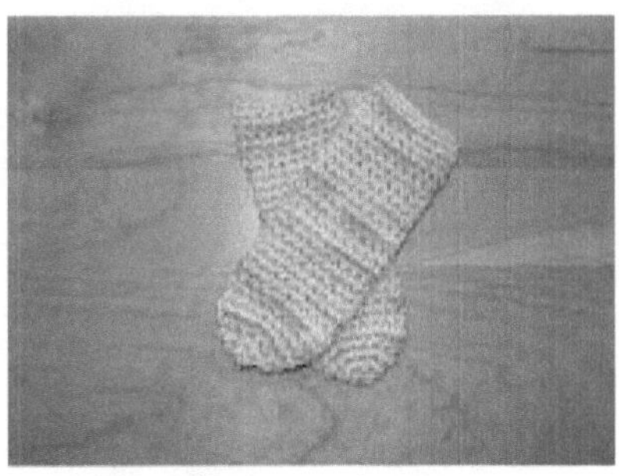

Materials

- Worsted Weight Yarn or Medium Cotton Yarn

- Crochet Hook size J or 6mm

- To change the size, use a smaller or larger hook

Directions

1. **Round 1-** Chain 2, working over the yarn tail, 8 single crochet in 2nd chain from the hook, pull yarn tail tight to close hole. **Round 2-** 2 single crochet in each single crochet. **Round 3-** Single crochet in next single crochet, 2 single crochet in next; repeat this all the way around. Join with a sl st to first single crochet.

2. **Round 4-** Chain 3, double crochet in each rem 23 double crochet. Join with a slip stich to beg double crochet. **Round 5-** Chain 3, 2 double crochet in same stitch, skip 2 stitches, single crochet in next stitch, skip 2 stitches, 5 double crochet in next stitch,

skip 2 stitches, single crochet in next stitch, skip 2 stitches, shell in next stitch, rep 2 more times, skip 2 stitches, 2 double crochet in same space as half shell to complete the shell. Join with a slip stitch to top of beg chain 3. Do not turn.

3. **Round 6-** Chain 1, single crochet in same space as joining, shell in next single crochet, *single crochet in 3rd double crochet of next shell, shell in next single crochet, rep from * 2 more times, join with a slip stitch to first stitch single crochet. Do not turn.

4. **Round 7-** Chain 3, 2 double crochet in same stitch; single crochet in 3rd double crochet of next shell, shell in next single crochet, repeat around, 2 double crochet in same space as beginning shell to complete shell, join with a slip stitch to top of beg chain 3. Do not turn.

5. **Round 8-** Repeat Round 6. **Round 9-** Repeat Round 7. **Round 10-** Rep Round 6. **Round 11-** Rep Round 7. **Round 12-** Rep Round 6.

6. **Round 13-** Chain 2, half double crochet in same space, half double crochet in each double crochet and single crochet around. Join with a slip stitch. Fasten off and weave in ends.

36. Soft Play and Nap Mat

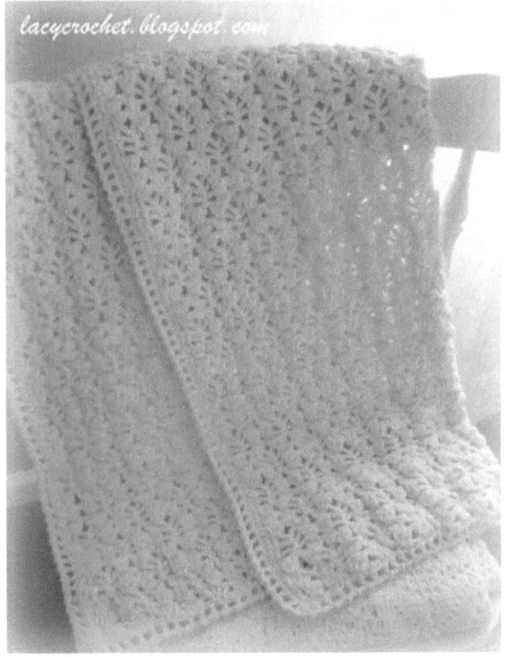

Materials

- 6 skeins of super bulky yarn in 3 colors, 2 skeins of each

- Crochet hook size N or 9mm

- Change colors wherever you like in the pattern

Directions

Cluster- To make a cluster work 2 double crochet, chain 3, 2 double crochet in the same stitch.

1. Chain 76.

2. **Row 1**- In the 6th chain from the hook, work a cluster all in the same chain. Skip 5 chains then in the next chain, work a cluster. Repeat this pattern until the last 4 chains. Skip 3 chains and in the last chain work a dc.

3. **Row 2**- Chain 3 and turn. Work a cluster into the center of each fan from the previous row all the way across. Work a dc in the turning chain space at the end. Repeat until the mat is the size that you want it to be.

37. Thick and Quick Crib Blanket

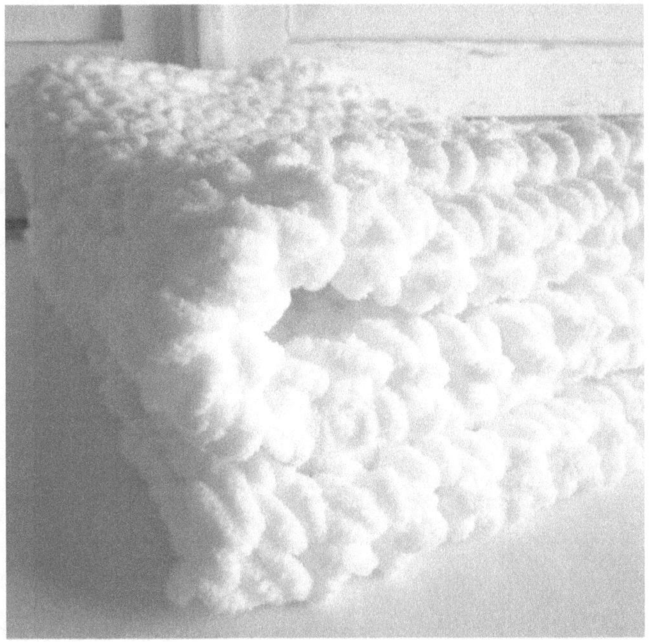

Materials

- Sport weight yarn in 4 different colors

- Crochet hook size N or 10mm

Directions

Note- To make this crib blanket you will be working with one strand of yarn in each color held together. So, you will be working with 4 strands of yarn total to make the entire blanket.

1. Chain 82.

2. **Row 1**- Singe crochet in 2nd chain from hook and in each chain across; turn.

3. **Row 2**- Chain 1, single crochet in each single crochet across; turn.

4. Repeat Row 2 until blanket measures approximately 40 inches long. Turn at the end of the final row.

Edging

1. **Round 1**- Chain 1, single crochet evenly around all 4 sides, working 3 single crochet in corners and taking care to keep work flat; join with a slip stitch to the first stitch.

2. **Round 2**- Chain 1, single crochet in first single crochet, chain 1, skip next sing crochet then single crochet in next single crochet, chain 1, repeat that all the way around making sure to work 3 single crochet in each corner. Fasten off and weave in ends.

38. Baby Bottle Holder

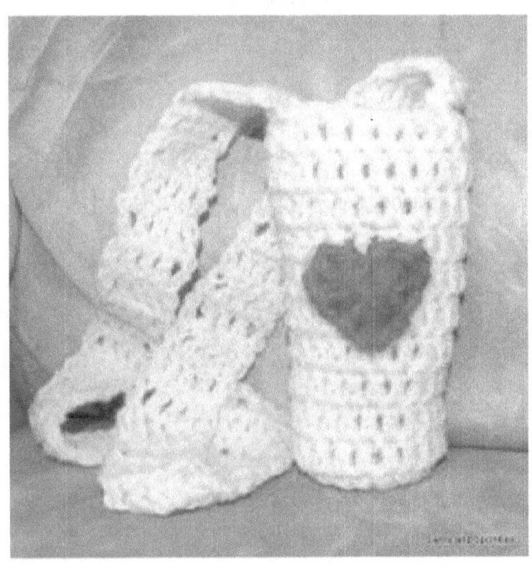

Materials

- Medium or chunky weight cotton yarn, any color

- Crochet hook size F

Directions

1. **Round 1-** Chain 27, join with slip stitch to form a ring being careful not to twist the chain.

2. **Round 2-** Chain 2, half double crochet in next stitch, triple crochet in next stitch. Half double crochet in next 2 stitches, triple crochet in next stitch. Repeat this pattern all the way around. Join with slip stitch in top of the beginning chain 2. Do not turn.

3. **Round 3-** Chain 1, half double crochet in each stitch around. Join with slip stitch in top of beginning chain 2. Do not turn.

4. **Rounds 4-7-** Repeat Row 3. **Round 8-** Repeat Row 2. **Rounds 9-13-** Repeat Row 3. **Round 14-** Repeat Row 2. **Round 15-** Repeat Row 3.

5. **Round 16-** Chain 2 more. Skip next stitch, single crochet in next stitch, chain 4. Repeat this pattern around.

6. **Finishing-** Attach yarn on opposite end, chain 2 then repeat Round 16. Fasten off.

Carrying Handle

1. Attach yarn to one side of the top opening with a slip stitch. Chain 100 or however long you want the handle to be. Attach with a slip stitch to the other side. Fasten off. Weave in all the end.

39. All-Natural Burp Cloth

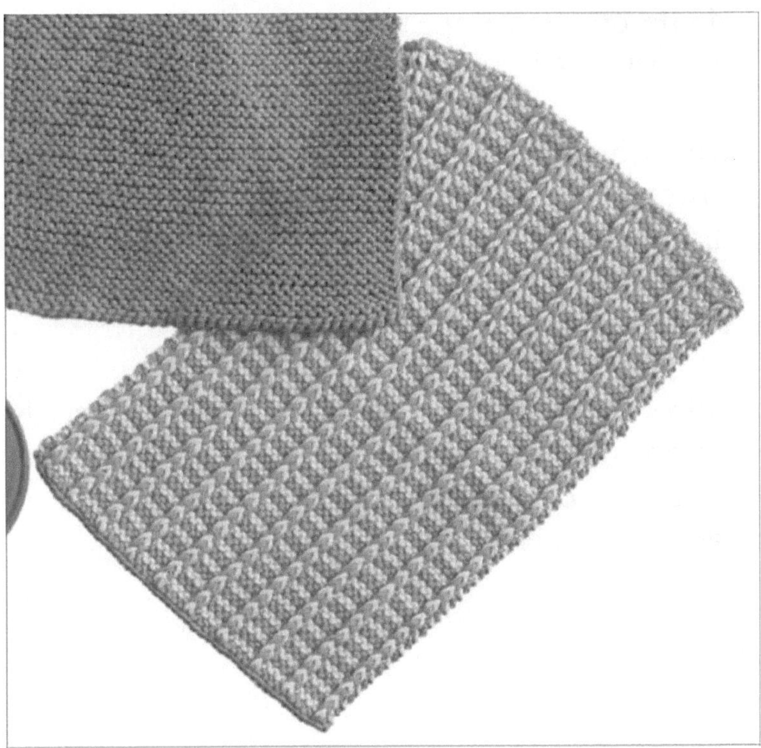

Materials

- Medium weight natural cotton yarn in any color

- Crochet hook size H

Directions

1. **Row 1-** Chain 31, single crochet in 2nd chain from hook, single crochet in each stitch across. Chain 1 and turn.

2. **Rows 2-** Skip first single crochet, 1 single crochet and 1 double crochet in the next stitch, skip the next single crochet. Repeat to the end. Single crochet in the last sc. Chain 2 and turn.

3. **Rows 3-** Skip to the single crochet from previous row, work 1 single crochet and 1 double crochet in that stitch, work 1 single crochet and 1 double crochet in each stitch until the end of the row. Single crochet in the last stitch. Chain 2 and turn.

4. **Rows 4-50-** Repeat Row 3. **Row 51-** Repeat Row 3 except only chain 1 at the end and turn. **Row 52-** Single crochet in each stitch across. Fasten off and weave in all ends.

40. Crib Rail Guards

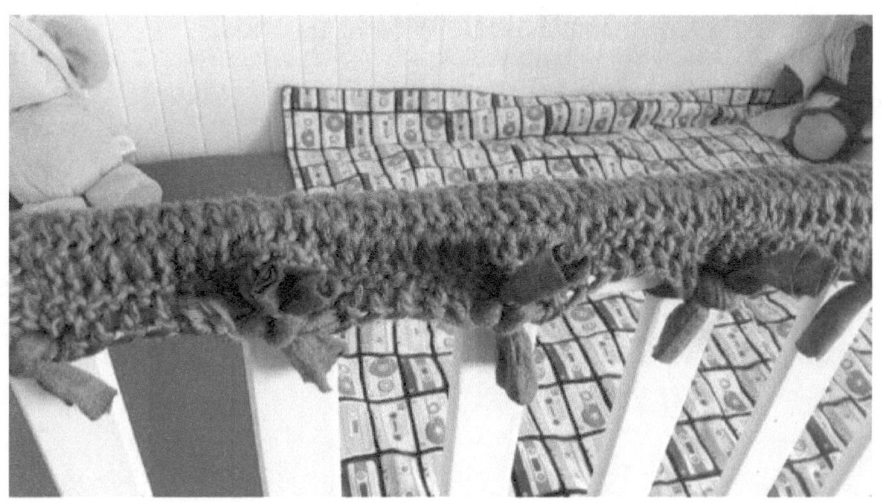

Materials

- Worsted weight baby yarn in any color

- 14-20 10-inch-long pieces of ribbon to tie the guards to the rails

- Crochet hook size H

Directions

1. Chain 16.

2. **Row 1-** Single crochet in the second chain from the hook. Single crochet all the way to the end. Chain 1, turn.

3. **Rows 2-20-** Repeat Row 1 until the piece of crocheted material is wide enough to go around your crib's rails. Fasten off. Weave in ends.

Finishing

1. Take the ribbons and thread a piece of ribbon through the crochet stitches to tie the crib guard around your crib's rails. Repeat this all along the length of the rail tying the piece down ever 4-6 inches.

41. Colorful Baby Blocks

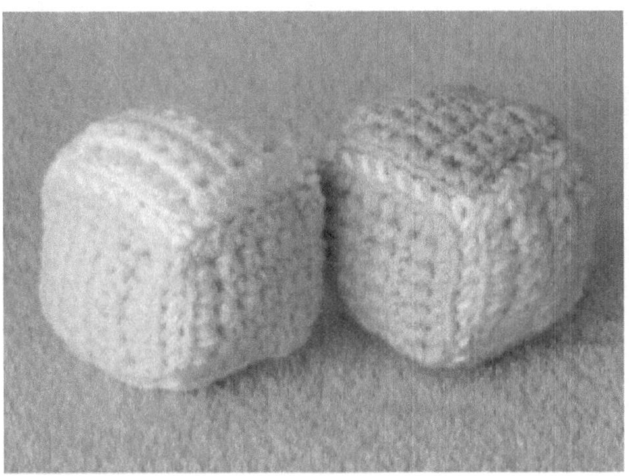

Materials

- Craft stuffing

- Crochet hook size F

- Worsted weight yarn in bright primary colors

Directions

Make 4 of these for each block. To make the blocks more eye-catching use different colors for each side of the block or use stripes or sew on letters or other appliques.

1. **Round 1-** chain 13.

2. **Round 2-** Single crochet in 2nd chain from hook, single crochet across and chain 1. Turn.

3. **Round 3-10-** Repeat Row 2.

4. Faster off. Weave in ends.

5. Sew three of the blocks together with one on the bottom and two sides to make a square. Stuff with craft stuffing. Then sew the final piece on the top to make a square block.

The projects in this book are especially designed with babies in mind. Each is a personal wish saying to this precious new life, "Welcome, I am so glad you are here."

Last Chance to Get YOUR Bonus!

FOR A LIMITED TIME ONLY – Get my best-selling book "DIY Crafts: The 100 Most Popular Crafts & Projects That Make Your Life Easier" absolutely FREE!

Readers who have downloaded the bonus book as well have seen the greatest changes in their crafting abilities and have expanded their repertoire of crafts – so it is *highly recommended* to get this bonus book today!

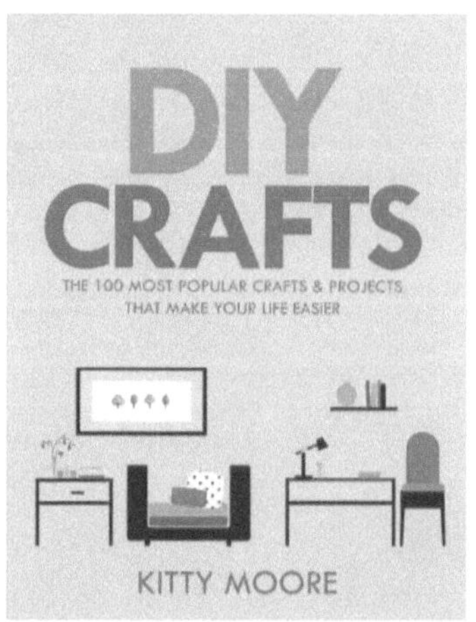

Get your free copy at:

ArtsCraftsAndMore.com/Bonus

Final Words

Thank you for downloading this book!

I really hope that you have been inspired to create your own projects and that you will have a lot of fun crafting.

I do hope that you and your family have found lots of ways to fill lazy afternoons or rainy days in a more fun way.

If you have enjoyed this book and would like to share your positive thoughts, could you please take 30 seconds of your time to go back and give me a review on my Amazon book page!

I really appreciate these reviews because I like to know what people have thought about the book.

Again, thank you and have fun crafting!

Disclaimer

No Warranties: The authors and publishers don't guarantee or warrant the quality, accuracy, completeness, timeliness, appropriateness or suitability of the information in this book, or of any product or services referenced by this site.

The information in this site is provided on an "as is" basis and the authors and publishers make no representations or warranties of any kind with respect to this information. This site may contain inaccuracies, typographical errors, or other errors.

Liability Disclaimer: The publishers, authors, and other parties involved in the creation, production, provision of information, or delivery of this site specifically disclaim any responsibility, and shall not be held liable for any damages, claims, injuries, losses, liabilities, costs, or obligations including any direct, indirect, special, incidental, or consequences damages (collectively known as "Damages") whatsoever and howsoever caused, arising out of, or in connection with the use or misuse of the site and the information contained within it, whether such Damages arise in contract, tort, negligence, equity, statute law, or by way of other legal theory.